Debilitated & D
Em

By

Anne Dryburgh

What Others are Saying About Debilitated and Diminished

"In this book, Dr. Dryburgh rings a cry for help for one of the most helpless people to walk the earth-the abused woman. There is no shortage of books on theology and culture, but it is rare to find one helping these women who have suffered terribly. Dr. Dryburgh speaks to these women and us in a clear and concise style as she elevates the Word of God and our need and responsibility to help these women."

Rev Johnny Touchet
Regional Mentor for International Association of Biblical Counselors
Trustee at The Southern Baptist Seminary in Louisville, KY
Pastor of Mount Moriah Baptist Church in Piedmont SC

"Anne Dryburgh has written an important book on a common counseling situation - emotionally abused wives. As common as it is, there are few resources that offer a biblical perspective on the topic. This book fills the gap and will benefit counselors and church leaders who serve emotionally abused women. The book gives us a comprehensive view of emotional abuse with the end goal of helping the wife to live a life pleasing to God as she navigates a difficult marriage. The definition of abuse is insightful and thorough. Counselors, pastors and elders will find this book to be full of scholarly wisdom and practical advice. I will be referring to this book for guidance as I serve women who are suffering from this form of abuse. This guidance will assure that the counseling approach is thorough."

Ellen Castillo Executive Director of Word of Hope Ministries, Inc.
IABC certified Biblical Counselor
Biblical Counseling Coalition Council Board Member

"Dr. Anne Dryburgh has produced a wonderful and biblical resource for women in abusive relationships and for those of us who help them. She tackles a very difficult subject with a balance of compassion and truth. Pastors will find this book contains biblical and practical ways for the church to minister to abused women, and counselors will learn the numerous heart issues behind abusive relationships. Most importantly,

Anne presents the biblical responses the abused woman should seek to build into her life. I am so excited about this new and excellent resource!"

Julie Ganschow MABC

Founder and Director of Reigning Grace Counseling Center (ACBC, IABC, AABC Certified Training Center) and Biblical Counseling for Women.
Association of Certified Biblical Counselors (ACBC), the International Association of Biblical Counselors (IABC), and the American Academy of Biblical Counselors (AABC) certified counselor.
Biblical Counseling Coalition Council Board Member

"There are scores of books in the marketplace for women of spousal abuse. Very few, however, are from a truly biblical perspective as is this book by my friend Anne Dryburgh. With great compassion and clarity she defines and describes emotional abuse and its impact on the life of the victim. She is careful to redefine and replace secular terms with biblical truth which will help the Christian view abuse and its effects the way God does. She is then able to provide the answers that guide the victim of emotional abuse in a redemptive walk with the Spirit to a new way of life that brings healing and purpose to the suffering she has endured. This is a book for victims, counselors and Church leaders alike and will help bring healing to the many hurting women in our midst with the Gospel of Christ. I heartily recommend it."

Dr. Bill Hines has a B.A. in Political Science, an M.A. each in Counseling and Religion from Liberty University, and a D.Min. in Biblical Counseling from Trinity Theological Seminary/University of Liverpool. He is the president of Covenant Ministries, a biblical counseling, education and Christian discipleship ministry in Ft. Worth, Texas. Bill is the author of *Leaving Yesterday Behind* and *Curing the Heart: A Model for Biblical Counseling* (with Dr. Howard Eyrich). He co-authored *The Pursuit of Perfection* with Mark Shaw and together with Mark Shaw edited *Paul the Counselor: Counseling and Disciple-Making Modeled by the Apostle.*

"Debilitated and Diminished, by Anne Dryburgh is greatly needed in the church today. Anne's writing is solidly biblical and deeply compassionate. Biblical counselors, pastors, church leaders, family, friends, and the emotionally abused woman will all benefit from Anne's practical wisdom."

Dr. Robert W. Kellemen, Chair of the Biblical Counseling Department at Crossroads Bible College, and Author of Sexual Abuse: Beauty for Ashes

TABLE OF CONTENTS

I.	Introduction:.	8
II.	Chapter One: Emotional Abuse Defined and its Debilitating Effects Described	15
III.	Chapter Two: The Impact of Sin and Christ's Work on Humanity and the Marital Relationship	49
IV.	Chapter Three: Living in Christ as the Wife of an Emotional Abuser	81
V.	Chapter Four: The Role of the Church	131
VI.	Chapter Five: Applying What we Have Learned	158
Bibliography		175

Introduction

Linda had given up. Depressed, listless, and lifeless, she lay on her bed all day every day. This was after years of being insulted, ridiculed, controlled, and punished by her husband Frank. While treating her in this way, he appeared to be spiritual to the other members of the church. When Frank left her for another woman, she gave up and spent the rest of her life in bed. That is when she went to Brian for help.

Louise is in her seventies. Her husband, Stephen, treats her the same as Frank treated Linda. Despite doing all she could to love and care for him, things have not improved. Stephen knows that he can treat his wife however he wants and he will always get his own way. Louise wonders what is wrong with her and why her husband won't love her. That is when she went to Brian for help.

Brian is a godly man and has been a church leader for decades. His father taught him the importance of caring for his family. Brian has been a living example of this. His life is a testimony to the loving care a husband and father is called to give. Being such a caring man, he struggles to understand why some husbands do not treat their wives well. When he heard Linda and Louise's stories, his heart was broken. He desperately wanted to help but since such behaviour was foreign to him, he knew he would have to thoroughly study scripture to gain insight into how to help these women know Christ in their situation. Brian believes in the sufficiency of Christ and scripture and that there must be answers in the Bible to help these women know and glorify the Lord in their suffering.

Frank and Stephen treat their wives in emotionally abusive ways. During the quarter of a century that I have been involved in discipleship and biblical counselling, my heart has been broken numerous times by hearing such stories. The suffering of these women has caused me to take this issue seriously, believing that there must be answers in the Bible for them to know the Lord in their situation. With my whole heart I was convinced that there must be better answers in scripture than the two typical answers that are given; submit or divorce. In order to ensure that the research I conducted was at the highest possible level, I studied it as my PhD dissertation topic. This book that is the result is designed to provide biblical insights for those who are helping women in emotionally abusive relationships.

In recent years the issue of abuse in marriage has gained international attention, especially physical violence and emotional abuse.[1] While considerable work has been conducted by researchers, little work has been done in the Christian world.

Often when the subject of abuse is addressed, there is a tendency to focus on physical abuse and certain issues that are involved.[2] Examples of such issues are hurt, rejection, fear,

---

[1]United Nations, "International Day for the Elimination of Violence Against Women," http://www.un.org/en/events/endviolenceday/ (accessed May 31, 2014); Beverly Engel, *The Emotionally Abusive Relationship: How to Stop Being Abused and How to Stop Abusing* (Hoboken: John Wiley & Sons Inc., 2002).

[2]George Scipione, "How to Counsel Spousal Abuse," *National Association of Nouthetic Counselors,* Conference 1999, CD N9938; Debi Pryde & Robert Needham, *A Biblical Perspective of What to Do When You are Abused by Your Husband* (New Springs: Iron Sharpeneth Iron Publications, 2003); Laura Hendrickson, "Counseling Victims of Spousal Abuse," *Institute for Biblical Counseling & Discipleship,* mp3, http://www.ibcd.org/resources/messages/counseling-victims-of-spousal-abuse/ (accessed January 16, 2014); Robert Kelleman, "Counseling and Abuse in Marriage," *RPM Ministries,* Pdf; John Street, "Handle with Care: Counseling Abuse Victims." *National Association of Nouthetic Counselors* Conference 2012, mp3; Wm Goode, "Wife Abuse (90)" *National Association of Nouthetic Counselors,* Annual Conference 1990, CD N9027; Sid Galloway, "Wife Abuse," *National Association of Nouthetic Counselors,* Annual Conference 1992, CD N9209; Robert Needham, "Abuse: Recognizing It," *Institute for Biblical Counseling & Discipleship,* mp3, http://www.soundword.com/ab1reitm.html (accessed January 16, 2014); Robert Needham, "Abuse: Addressing It." *Institute for Biblical Counseling & Discipleship,* mp3, February 10th, 2013 http:ibcd.org/resources/messages/cdc1-14-1angerabuse/ (accessed January 16, 2014).

anger, forgiveness, and shame.³ It is common for well-intentioned counsellors to advise women to submit to their husbands unless they are asked to sin or are being physically abused.⁴ This approach, however, does not address how submission in some non-sin areas can lead to wives being controlled and manipulated by their husbands in emotionally abusive relationships.

Clearly, there is need for a comprehensive biblical view about how to counsel Christian women in emotionally abusive marriages so that they can live lives that glorify Christ in their situations. The purpose of this book is to provide a resource to use when counselling Christian women who are being treated in an emotionally abusive manner by their husbands. It does not

---

³Lou Priolo, "How to Respond to Rejection and Hurt," *The Lou Priolo Library*, CD LP52b; Lou Priolo, "Helping People Pleasers," *National Association of Nouthetic Counselors*, Conference 2006, mp3; Ed Welch, *When People are Big and God is Small: Overcoming Peer Pressure, Codependency, and the Fear of Man* (Phillipsburg: P&R Publishing, 1997); Jim Newheiser, "Anger/Abuse," *Institute for Biblical Counseling & Discipleship*, mp3, February 10th, 2013. http://www.ibcd.org/resources/messages/cdc1-14-angerabuse/ (accessed January 16, 2014); Lou Priolo, "Counseling Angry People," *The Institute for Biblical Counseling & Discipleship*, mp3, June 26th, 2008. Pryde & Needham, *A Biblical Perspective of What to Do When You are Abused By Your Husband;* Priolo, "How to Respond to Rejection & Hurt," Newheiser, "Anger. Abuse."; Hendrickson, "Counseling Victims of Spousal Abuse," Priolo, "Counseling Angry People," Robert Kelleman, *Sexual Abuse: Beauty for Ashes* (Phillipsburg: P&R Publishing, 2013); Needham, "Abuse Recognizing It."http://www.ibcd.org/resources/messages/counseling-angry-people/ (accessed January 17, 2014); Galloway, "Wife Abuse."; Ed Welch, *Shame Interrupted: How God Lifts the Pain of Worthlessness & Rejection* (Greensboro: New Growth Press, 2012).

⁴Martha Peace, "Counseling Women to be Godly Wives," *National Association of Nouthetic Counselors* Conference 2013.

cover physical or sexual abuse in marriage and it assumes that the position of headship is one of authority.

When you set out to help someone, it is important to gain as much information about the person's situation as you can. The first chapter provides such information by explaining the dynamics of emotional abuse. This is done by defining this type of abuse, describing the typical behaviours that emotionally abusive husbands engage in and the typical ways in which the wives respond. This provides you with insight into the issues and the kind of relational dynamics that you can expect when seeking to help her.

Since you are seeking to help her know Christ and to live in a God-honouring way, it is essential to understand what God says about who she is as a woman. The second chapter explores what it means to be made in the image of God, the effects of the Fall on the marital relationship, what it means to be renewed in Christ, and headship and submission in marriage.

Building on the foundation laid in chapter two, chapter three provides concrete ways of helping emotionally abused women. It covers their purpose in life, their identity, the issue of submission in an emotionally abusive relationship, issues that abused women usually suffer from, how to honour Christ in the home, and the importance of the church.

Chapter four explains what the church is and the important role that it plays in helping the woman. The fifth, and last, chapter takes what has been learned and provides suggestions about how these insights can be applied when helping emotionally abused women.

The Need for Caution and Wisdom

A word of caution is necessary. Abusive situations are gravely serious. While insights have been suggested in this book, it is not the definitive answer about how to help abused women. It touches on subjects that are tremendously complicated and where time is needed to address these areas in an in-depth manner to be able to effectively help people. Well-intentioned, but unwise, advice can cause suffering and damage lives. Wisdom and insight are required when you help each individual involved. There are no standard, cut-and-dried, answers.

Chapter One

Hannah was the courageous one. Deep down, she knew that something just was not right about her marriage. Ever since their wedding, she had accepted that she was to blame for their difficulties. At the time, she decided that she would love her husband even more. This would hopefully make him less angry and be beneficial to their relationship. As a Christian wife, she consciously chose to be submissive to his decisions and wishes. Yet things kept getting worse. David wanted her to stay in the house all day. She was not allowed any friends over to visit. Whenever she did something he perceived to be wrong, there would be a torrent of insults about how bad a wife she was. After adapting to his expectations, there would be another torrent of insults, this time demanding that she be who she was in the first place. Hannah was fearful, hurt, angry, and aware that she was heading toward depression.

A Definition of Emotional Abuse

Conflict happens in every marriage, but there is a difference between an abusive relationship and one that is going through a time of difficulty. Verbally assaulting a spouse during an argument does not make the relationship abusive.[5] An emotionally abusive relationship is one in which one partner exhibits a consistent pattern of behaviour that is designed to control the other.[6] The victim responds to the abusive behaviour by becoming dependent upon the abuser.[7]

Emotional abuse can be defined as: Emotional abuse is any non-physical behaviour that is designed to control, intimidate, subjugate, punish, or isolate another person resulting in the

---

[5]Marti Loring, *Emotional Abuse* (San Francisco: Jossey-Bass Publishers, 1994), 2.

[6]Ibid.; Brittney Nicols, "Violence Against Women: The Extent of the Problem," In *"Intimate Violence Against Women: When Spouses, Partners, or Lovers Attack,* edited by Paula Lundberg-Love and Shelly Marmion, (Westport: Praeger Publishers, 2006); Beverly Engel, *The Emotionally Abused Woman: Overcoming Destructive Patterns and Reclaiming Yourself* (New York: Fawcett Books, 1990), 22; Loring, *Emotional Abuse* (San Francisco: Jossey-Bass Publishers, 1994), 2; Engel, *The Emotionally Abused Woman: Overcoming Destructive Patterns and Reclaiming Yourself,* 22, 47; Mary Miller, *No Visible Wounds: Identifying Nonphysical Abuse of Women by their Men* (New York: Ballantine Books, 1995), 15; Evan Stark, *Coercive Control: How Men Entrap Women in Personal Life* (New York: Oxford University Press, 2007), 228; Diane Follingstad and Dana Dehart, "Defining Psychological Abuse of Husbands Toward Wives Contexts, Behaviors, and Typologies," *Journal of Interpersonal Violence* 15, no. 9 (September 2000): 891-920.

[7]Miller, *No Visible Wounds: Identifying Nonphysical Abuse of Women by their Men,* 25; Stark, *Coercive Control: How Men Entrap Women in Personal Life,* 228.

victim becoming emotionally, behaviourally, and mentally dependent on the abuser.[8]

Although the intent and the outcome of the abuse can be discerned, there is little agreement about what actual behaviours are involved.[9] However, certain types of behaviour and responses are common for both the abuser and the abused. Common behaviours that abusers engage in are: verbal abuse, coercion and threats, minimizing, denying, and blaming, intimidation, mind games, isolation, male privilege, financial control, using the children, exhibiting two different personalities, jealousy, and good periods. These behaviours work together to lead to the abuser having control over the victim. However, not every abuser uses all of these behaviours. There are also common responses to and effects of emotional abuse on the victims. These are: confusion, doubt, fear, guilt, worry, inhibition, anger, shame, a changed mental state,

---

[8]This definition is an expansion of Engel's definition in Beverly Engel, *The Emotionally Abusive Relationship: How to Stop Being Abused and How to Stop Abusing* (Hoboken: John Wiley & Sons Inc., 2002), 10. This definition includes the effect of emotional abuse on the victim.

[9]Diane Follingstad and Dana Dehart, "Defining Psychological Abuse of Husbands Toward Wives Contexts, Behaviors, and Typologies," *Journal of Interpersonal Violence* 15, no. 9 (September 2000): 891-920.

emotional, behavioural, and mental dependence upon the abuser, physical ailments, loneliness, depression, and sorrow.

A Description of Emotional Abuse

Verbal Abuse

Verbal abuse involves speaking in an attacking or hurtful way, with the purpose of leading someone to believe something that is not true, or to speak to another in a way that is not true.[10] It involves overt and covert behaviour.[11]

Overt abuse is "openly demeaning" behaviour that includes belittling, yelling, name-calling, criticizing, ordering around, sulking, accusing, ridiculing, insulting, trivializing, expressing disgust toward the victim, threatening, blaming, humiliating,

---

[10]Patricia Evans, *The Verbally Abusive Relationship: How to Recognize it and How to Respond* (Avon, MA: Adams Media, 2010), 77.

[11]Ibid.

shouting, and shaming.[12]

Covert abuse is subtle. The victim is aware that something is wrong but is not certain what the actual problem is.[13] It includes discounting, negating, accusing, denying, labelling, using subtle threats, disapproving facial expressions, and sarcastic tone of voice, implying that the victim is inadequate, joking to diminish the victim, interrupting the victim, and twisting and distorting what the victim says.[14]

When calling the victim names, words are spoken that attack a woman's humanity, femininity, and even lower her to the status of

---

[12]Loring, *Emotional Abuse*, 3; Nicols, "Violence Against Women: The Extent of the Problem," In *"Intimate Violence Against Women: When Spouses, Partners, or Lovers Attack,* edited by Paula Lundberg-Love and Shelly Marmion, 16-17; Albert Ellis and Marcia Powers, *The Secret of Overcoming Verbal Abuse: Getting Off the Emotional Roller Coaster and Regaining Control of Your Life* (Hollywood: Wilshire Book Company, 2000), 18; Lundy Bancroft, *Why Does he Do That?: Inside the Minds of Angry and Controlling Men* (New York: Berkley Books, 2002), 144-145; Evans, *The Verbally Abusive Relationship: How to Recognize it and How to Respond,* 95; Engel, *The Emotionally Abused Woman: Overcoming Destructive Patterns and Reclaiming Yourself,* 47.

[13]Ellis and Powers, *The Secret of Overcoming Verbal Abuse: Getting Off the Emotional Roller Coaster and Regaining Control of Your Life,* 16.

[14]Loring, *Emotional Abuse*, 3; Nicols, "Violence Against Women: The Extent of the Problem," In *"Intimate Violence Against Women: When Spouses, Partners, or Lovers Attack,* edited by Paula Lundberg-Love and Shelly Marmion, 17-18; Ellis and Powers, *The Secret of Overcoming Verbal Abuse: Getting Off the Emotional Roller Coaster and Regaining Control of Your Life,* 16-18; Engel, *The Emotionally Abused Woman: Overcoming Destructive Patterns and Reclaiming Yourself,* 23; Marie-France Hirigoyen, *Stalking the Soul: Emotional Abuse and the Erosion of Identity* (New York: Helen Marx Books, 2004), 100.

an animal or a part of the human body.[15] The abuser may use technical language which the victim does not understand.[16]

Coercion and Threats

An emotionally abusive husband will usually threaten his wife.[17] Threats are used in relation to things on which the woman depends, such as food, money, clothing, medicine, and the children. He may also threaten to withdraw emotionally, to ignore her, and even to commit suicide.[18]

Coercive control is used while trying to frighten the victim. Examples of such control mechanisms are leaving anonymous threats on an answering machine, removing clothing or memorabilia,

---

[15]Bancroft, *Why Does he Do That?: Inside the Minds of Angry and Controlling Men*, 63; Evans, *The Verbally Abusive Relationship: How to Recognize it and How to Respond*, 77; Hirigoyen, *Stalking the Soul: Emotional Abuse and the Erosion of Identity*, 104.

[16]Hirigoyen, *Stalking the Soul: Emotional Abuse and the Erosion of Identity*, 99.

[17]Loring, *Emotional Abuse*, 43; Nicols, "Violence Against Women: The Extent of the Problem," In *"Intimate Violence Against Women: When Spouses, Partners, or Lovers Attack*, edited by Paula Lundberg-Love and Shelly Marmion, 6; Engel, *The Emotionally Abused Woman: Overcoming Destructive Patterns and Reclaiming Yourself*, 47; Miller, *No Visible Wounds: Identifying Nonphysical Abuse of Women by their Men*, 47; Ginny NiCarthy, *Getting Free: A Handbook for Women in Abusive Situations* (Worcester: Billing & Sons, Ltd., 1991), 231-234; Stark, *Coercive Control: How Men Entrap Women in Personal Life*, 228.

[18]Ibid., 253.

cutting telephone wires, slashing tires, and stealing post.[19] The abuser may use secrets that she has told him to his own advantage and behave in an embarrassing way in public.[20] The wife can never know whether or not he will carry out the threats, resulting in her living in a state of anxiety, despair, and helplessness.[21] The abuser is then able to control every detail of her daily life, even to the extent of what they eat, when, where, and how she drives a car, how she dresses, how she cleans herself, and what she watches on television.[22]

Minimizing, Denying, and Blaming

Minimizing occurs when the abuser attempts to invalidate the victim's feelings or how the victim experiences reality.[23] It includes

---

[19]Ibid., 254.

[20]Ibid., 50; Miller, *No Visible Wounds: Identifying Nonphysical Abuse of Women by their Men*, 255.

[21]NiCarthy, *Getting Free: A Handbook for Women in Abusive Situations*, 231, 234; Miller, *No Visible Wounds: Identifying Nonphysical Abuse of Women by their Men*, 47; Engel, *The Emotionally Abused Woman: Overcoming Destructive Patterns and Reclaiming Yourself*, 47.

[22]Stark, *Coercive Control: How Men Entrap Women in Personal Life*, 274.

[23]Evans, *The Verbally Abusive Relationship: How to Recognize it and How to Respond*, 25, 46.

trivializing and discounting what the victim thinks and does.[24] He might discount her achievements because he is trying to keep control of her.[25]

The perpetrator might deny that the abuse has happened, what he is clearly feeling, or the truth or realness of the victim's "thoughts, perceptions, or feelings." He may claim that he knows these better than the victim herself.[26]

The abuser will blame the victim for his own behaviour.[27] By doing so, he avoids dealing with the situation that is bothering him

---

[24]Ibid., 190.

[25]Nicols, "Violence Against Women: The Extent of the Problem," In *"Intimate Violence Against Women: When Spouses, Partners, or Lovers Attack,* edited by Paula Lundberg-Love and Shelly Marmion, 17.

[26]Loring, *Emotional Abuse,* 39; Nicols, "Violence Against Women: The Extent of the Problem," In *"Intimate Violence Against Women: When Spouses, Partners, or Lovers Attack,* edited by Paula Lundberg-Love and Shelly Marmion, 17; Bancroft, *Why Does he Do That?: Inside the Minds of Angry and Controlling Men,* 63, 66, 40; Evans, *The Verbally Abusive Relationship: How to Recognize it and How to Respond,* 17, 38, 191, 192; Ellis and Powers, *The Secret of Overcoming Verbal Abuse: Getting Off the Emotional Roller Coaster and Regaining Control of Your Life,* 17.

[27]Bancroft, *Why Does he Do That?: Inside the Minds of Angry and Controlling Men,* 18; Evans, *The Verbally Abusive Relationship: How to Recognize it and How to Respond,* 173; Engel, *The Emotionally Abused Woman: Overcoming Destructive Patterns and Reclaiming Yourself,* 29; NiCarthy, *Getting Free: A Handbook for Women in Abusive Situations,* 234; Nicols, "Violence Against Women: The Extent of the Problem," In *"Intimate Violence Against Women: When Spouses, Partners, or Lovers Attack,* edited by Paula Lundberg-Love and Shelly Marmion, 17.

and the associated feelings.[28] He is therefore able to make her responsible for his actions.[29] By blaming the victim, he is able to prevent being confronted about himself.[30]

The victim is blamed because the abuser believes that she exists to make him happy. If he is not happy, he believes that it is the fault of the partner.[31] Using minimizing, denying, and blaming is an attempt to control the victim's thinking so that it conforms to that of his reality.[32]

Intimidation

Emotionally abusive men use intimidation to control circumstances or to cause their partners to live in fear or

---

[28]Nicols, "Violence Against Women: The Extent of the Problem," In *"Intimate Violence Against Women: When Spouses, Partners, or Lovers Attack,* edited by Paula Lundberg-Love and Shelly Marmion, 17.

[29]Bancroft, *Why Does he Do That?: Inside the Minds of Angry and Controlling Men,* 69.

[30]Ibid., 18.

[31]Evans, *The Verbally Abusive Relationship: How to Recognize it and How to Respond,* 173.

[32]Bancroft, *Why Does he Do That?: Inside the Minds of Angry and Controlling Men,* 49.

helplessness.[33] Intimidation can include getting too close to her when he is angry, blocking her way, claiming that his behaviour is an attempt to make her listen, or driving irresponsibly.[34] The three most common intimidating behaviours used are threats, surveillance, and degradation.[35] Due to living in a state of fear, the wife allows herself to be controlled, even though she has not suffered physical abuse. This is because she imagines what could possibly happen to her.[36]

Mind Games

The emotional abuser makes his victim doubt her own thinking. By doing this, she becomes dependent on him.[37] Various tricks are involved in the process. He may make remarks that cause confusion. Examples are "I am telling you this for your own good,"

---

[33]Ibid., 66, 119; Engel, *The Emotionally Abused Woman: Overcoming Destructive Patterns and Reclaiming Yourself,* 47; Stark, *Coercive Control: How Men Entrap Women in Personal Life,* 249.

[34]Bancroft, *Why Does he Do That?: Inside the Minds of Angry and Controlling Men,* 119.

[35]Stark, *Coercive Control: How Men Entrap Women in Personal Life,* 249.

[36]Ibid., 249, 251.

[37]Engel, *The Emotionally Abused Woman: Overcoming Destructive Patterns and Reclaiming Yourself,* 11.

"that never happened," and "you are just imagining it."[38] The subject of conversation may be overtly or covertly changed, he may be adamant that she is thinking things that she is not, and twist what she says.[39] At times he may be charming toward others, causing her to doubt whether someone who is so nice could be so bad.[40] Accusations that she has an evil character can lead her to become confused and to doubt her trust in her own thinking and values.[41] At this point she accepts the abuser's judgments of her as being true.[42]

"Gaslighting" or "gaslamping" is a common trick. This is when the abuser corrodes the foundation of logic upon which the victim thinks. It comes from the 1940 film *Gaslight,* based on the play by Patrick Hamilton. In the film, the culprit causes his

---

[38]Ellis and Powers, *The Secret of Overcoming Verbal Abuse: Getting Off the Emotional Roller Coaster and Regaining Control of Your Life,* 18.

[39]Bancroft, *Why Does he Do That?: Inside the Minds of Angry and Controlling Men,* 66.

[40]Ellis and Powers, *The Secret of Overcoming Verbal Abuse: Getting Off the Emotional Roller Coaster and Regaining Control of Your Life,* 22.

[41]Loring, *Emotional Abuse,* 5; Bancroft, *Why Does he Do That?: Inside the Minds of Angry and Controlling Men,* 22; NiCarthy, *Getting Free: A Handbook for Women in Abusive Situations,* 236.

[42]Loring, *Emotional Abuse,* 44; NiCarthy, *Getting Free: A Handbook for Women in Abusive Situations,* 236.

victim to doubt her own perceptions by adjusting the levels of light given by the gas lamps. For example, he may call her and give her instructions to pick something up for him, but later deny that he has called her. Or he may not call her and ask her why she did not do as he asked.[43] Or, he tells her that he likes his steak to be well-done after having told her that he always likes his steaks rare.[44] Things might be taken from her for an unknown reason, only to reappear after she has spent a long time looking for them.[45] The result of these behaviours is that she thinks that she is losing her mind.[46]

Isolation

An abuser usually isolates his partner by removing her support system of friends and family.[47] He believes that she should be there

---

[43]Miller, *No Visible Wounds: Identifying Nonphysical Abuse of Women by their Men*, 34.

[44]NiCarthy, *Getting Free: A Handbook for Women in Abusive Situations*, 236.

[45]Stark, *Coercive Control: How Men Entrap Women in Personal Life*, 255.

[46]Bancroft, *Why Does he Do That?: Inside the Minds of Angry and Controlling Men*, 66.

[47]Nicols, "Violence Against Women: The Extent of the Problem," In *"Intimate Violence Against Women: When Spouses, Partners, or Lovers Attack,* edited by Paula Lundberg-Love and Shelly Marmion, 33; Evans, *The Verbally Abusive Relationship: How to Recognize it and How to Respond,* 19; Hirigoyen, *Stalking the Soul: Emotional Abuse and the Erosion of Identity,* 231; Stark, *Coercive Control: How Men Entrap Women in Personal Life,* 5.

only for his needs and because others might help her become more independent and stronger.[48] He does this by complaining when she has contact with others, shaming or embarrassing her in front of others, engaging in stalking behaviours, moving her to a remote location, or forbidding her to leave the home.[49] Once she is isolated, he is able to give her wrong information, which cannot be corrected by others in her life. In this way, she becomes mentally dependent upon him.[50]

Male Privilege

In order for abuse to occur, there must be inequality in the relationship. In an emotionally abusive marriage, the wife is seen as

---

[48]Bancroft, *Why Does he Do That?: Inside the Minds of Angry and Controlling Men*, 52; Miller, *No Visible Wounds: Identifying Nonphysical Abuse of Women by their Men*, 44, 54; NiCarthy, *Getting Free: A Handbook for Women in Abusive Situations*, 109; Stark, *Coercive Control: How Men Entrap Women in Personal Life*, 262.

[49]Engel, *The Emotionally Abused Woman: Overcoming Destructive Patterns and Reclaiming Yourself*, 23; Miller, *No Visible Wounds: Identifying Nonphysical Abuse of Women by their Men*, 57; Nicols, "Violence Against Women: The Extent of the Problem," In *"Intimate Violence Against Women: When Spouses, Partners, or Lovers Attack*, edited by Paula Lundberg-Love and Shelly Marmion, 33; Ellis and Powers, *The Secret of Overcoming Verbal Abuse: Getting Off the Emotional Roller Coaster and Regaining Control of Your Life*, 19; Miller, *No Visible Wounds: Identifying Nonphysical Abuse of Women by their Men*, 59.

[50]NiCarthy, *Getting Free: A Handbook for Women in Abusive Situations*, 233, 236; Stark, *Coercive Control: How Men Entrap Women in Personal Life*, 262.

inferior by her husband.[51] This inferiority is with regard to her gender, intelligence, and logic.[52] Since masculinity is understood to involve control and dominance, he is able to control her as it is considered unfeminine to doubt or question his instructions.[53] She is expected to allow him to make decisions, while fulfilling her womanly role of cooking, cleaning, and caring for the children.[54] Her position in life is like that of an "unpaid servant."[55]

---

[51]Stark, *Coercive Control: How Men Entrap Women in Personal Life*, 5; Nicols, "Violence Against Women: The Extent of the Problem," In *"Intimate Violence Against Women: When Spouses, Partners, or Lovers Attack,* edited by Paula Lundberg-Love and Shelly Marmion, 32; Evans, *The Verbally Abusive Relationship: How to Recognize it and How to Respond*, 41.

[52]Bancroft, *Why Does he Do That?: Inside the Minds of Angry and Controlling Men*, 63.

[53]Ibid., 58.

[54]Stark, *Coercive Control: How Men Entrap Women in Personal Life*, 210; Nicols, "Violence Against Women: The Extent of the Problem," In *"Intimate Violence Against Women: When Spouses, Partners, or Lovers Attack,* edited by Paula Lundberg-Love and Shelly Marmion, 32; Bancroft, *Why Does he Do That?: Inside the Minds of Angry and Controlling Men*, 55.

[55] Bancroft, *Why Does he Do That?: Inside the Minds of Angry and Controlling Men*, 55.

Financial Control

Emotional abusers often do not give their wives enough money to be able to pay their daily expenses.[56] While depriving her of the needed money, he spends a lot of it on himself.[57] If she had her own bank account before she got married, he makes her give it to him.[58] If she has a job, he makes her give her income to him.[59] Family assets are put in his name. He may require a detailed account of everything that she has spent, accompany her when she has to spend money, and require that permission is given by him before she spends any money.[60] If he is displeased with her, he might remove her access to money, even if she has a legitimate claim to it.[61] Since she could not survive financially without him, she is under his

---

[56]Nicols, "Violence Against Women: The Extent of the Problem," In *"Intimate Violence Against Women: When Spouses, Partners, or Lovers Attack,* edited by Paula Lundberg-Love and Shelly Marmion, 32; Miller, *No Visible Wounds: Identifying Nonphysical Abuse of Women by their Men,* 70; Stark, *Coercive Control: How Men Entrap Women in Personal Life,* 5, 272.

[57]Evans, *The Verbally Abusive Relationship: How to Recognize it and How to Respond,* 193.

[58]Miller, *No Visible Wounds: Identifying Nonphysical Abuse of Women by their Men,* 71.

[59]Ibid.

[60]Stark, *Coercive Control: How Men Entrap Women in Personal Life,* 272.

[61]Ibid.

control.[62]

Using the Children

Since the emotionally abused woman cannot survive financially on her own, she will put up with the abuse so that she can care for her children.[63] When abusers sense that they are losing power over their wives, they often begin to verbally abuse the children. Their hurt causes her emotional distress.[64] The husband might demand much from the children and punish them when they fail, threaten them, or say that he will harm them.[65]

---

[62]Miller, *No Visible Wounds: Identifying Nonphysical Abuse of Women by their Men*, 70.

[63]Engel, *The Emotionally Abused Woman: Overcoming Destructive Patterns and Reclaiming Yourself*, 12.

[64]Miller, *No Visible Wounds: Identifying Nonphysical Abuse of Women by their Men*, 30.

[65]Nicols, "Violence Against Women: The Extent of the Problem," In *"Intimate Violence Against Women: When Spouses, Partners, or Lovers Attack,* edited by Paula Lundberg-Love and Shelly Marmion, 6, 32; Miller, *No Visible Wounds: Identifying Nonphysical Abuse of Women by their Men*, 47.

Having Two Personalities

Emotional abusers are often well-liked by other people. Outsiders may think that they are upstanding citizens.[66] They are able to relate to outsiders or colleagues in what is seen to be a mature way.[67] He may be calm with outsiders while being an angry man at home, be giving toward outsiders and selfish at home, or promote women's rights with outsiders while being derogatory toward women at home.[68] Since outsiders believe that he is an upstanding citizen, she knows that others will probably not believe her or may think that the situation is her fault.[69]

---

[66]Nicols, "Violence Against Women: The Extent of the Problem," In *Intimate Violence Against Women: When Spouses, Partners, or Lovers Attack,* edited by Paula Lundberg-Love and Shelly Marmion, 3; Bancroft, *Why Does he Do That?: Inside the Minds of Angry and Controlling Men,* 8; Miller, *No Visible Wounds: Identifying Nonphysical Abuse of Women by their Men,* 206.

[67]Bancroft, *Why Does he Do That?: Inside the Minds of Angry and Controlling Men,* 32.

[68]Ibid., 68.

[69]Ibid., 69.

Jealousy

Emotional abusers are usually jealous.[70] This is expressed by expecting that his wife prove her love for him, while being possessive toward her.[71] He might demand that she gives all her attention to him or accuse her of being interested in other men, when there is no reason to suspect this.[72] The jealousy, possession, and suspicion can lead to him stalking her. The stalking could involve calling her several times a day, expecting her to spend all her free time with him, or checking what she does with her time.[73] Any achievement made by his wife is seen as competition and as a threat to him.[74]

---

[70]Beverly Engel, *The Emotionally Abusive Relationship: How to Stop Being Abused and How to Stop Abusing* (Hoboken: John Wiley & Sons Inc., 2002), 26.
[71]Bancroft, *Why Does he Do That?: Inside the Minds of Angry and Controlling Men*, 41.

[72]Beverly Engel,*The Emotionally Abusive Relationship: How to Stop Being Abused and How to Stop Abusing,* 26, 190; Bancroft, *Why Does he Do That?: Inside the Minds of Angry and Controlling Men,* 73, 86; Stark, *Coercive Control: How Men Entrap Women in Personal Life,* 248.

[73]Bancroft, *Why Does he Do That?: Inside the Minds of Angry and Controlling Men,* 117.

[74]Evans, *The Verbally Abusive Relationship: How to Recognize it and How to Respond,* 43.

Good Periods

After a period of treating his wife badly, the abuser might begin to treat her well. Subsequent to expressing regret about his bad behaviour, there is a period when he is kind, generous, and loving. This leads her to hope that he is changing. As a result, she starts to invest in the relationship again.[75] His behaviour reminds her of the person that she fell in love with. She starts to trust him and becomes vulnerable again.[76] These good periods are, however, part of his abusive behaviour, they are not a change from it.[77]

The Effects of Emotional Abuse on the Victim

The various behaviours that have been described have a number of effects upon the victim of emotional abuse. As is the case with the abusive behaviours, the effects are linked to each other.

---

[75]NiCarthy, *Getting Free: A Handbook for Women in Abusive Situations*, 235.

[76]Bancroft, *Why Does he Do That?: Inside the Minds of Angry and Controlling Men*, 147.

[77]Ibid., 170.

Confusion

When a wife is emotionally abused by her husband, she becomes confused.[78] This is his intention, because it is then easier to manipulate her.[79] It is typical for the wife to examine all that has happened so that she can find something wrong with her that caused the abuse. She believes that knowing this will prevent it happening in the future.[80] However, his behaviours are too confusing for her to be able to see where she is wrong. For example, he might change the subject of the conversation or be adamant that she is thinking and feeling things which she is not.[81] He might declare his love to her verbally, while behaving toward her in a manner that expresses dislike.[82] When he is with outsiders he might behave well, yet be

---

[78]Ibid., 76; Ellis and Powers, *The Secret of Overcoming Verbal Abuse: Getting Off the Emotional Roller Coaster and Regaining Control of Your Life*, 25.

[79]Ellis and Powers, *The Secret of Overcoming Verbal Abuse: Getting Off the Emotional Roller Coaster and Regaining Control of Your Life*, 34.

[80]Loring, *Emotional Abuse*, 39; Evans, *The Verbally Abusive Relationship: How to Recognize it and How to Respond*, 63.

[81]Bancroft, *Why Does he Do That?: Inside the Minds of Angry and Controlling Men*, 67; Evans, *The Verbally Abusive Relationship: How to Recognize it and How to Respond*, 55.

[82]Bancroft, *Why Does he Do That?: Inside the Minds of Angry and Controlling Men*, 76; Evans, *The Verbally Abusive Relationship: How to Recognize it and How to Respond*, 38, 108, 195.

abusive toward her.[83] It is common for abusers to deny that he has said or done what he has clearly said or done.[84] If she accepts what he says as true, she is allowing him to define her experience. This will lead to even more confusion.[85]

Doubt

The emotional abuser wants the victim to doubt herself.[86] This is done by getting her to doubt her perceptions and thinking ability.[87] He might say things like, "You are just angry because you are not getting your own way, so you are saying that I am mistreating you."[88] He might say that she is illogical, wanting to be argumentative, is being selfish, and/or always has to have her own

---

[83]Bancroft, *Why Does he Do That?: Inside the Minds of Angry and Controlling Men*, 76.

[84]Loring, *Emotional Abuse*, 39; Evans, *The Verbally Abusive Relationship: How to Recognize it and How to Respond*, 38.

[85]Evans, *The Verbally Abusive Relationship: How to Recognize it and How to Respond*, 55; Rachel Novsak, Tina Mandelj, and Barbara Simonic, "Therapeutic Implications of Religious-Related Emotional Abuse," *Journal of Aggression, Maltreatment, & Trauma* Vol. 21, Issue 1 (2012): 31-44.

[86]Hirigoyen, *Stalking the Soul: Emotional Abuse and the Erosion of Identity*, 31, 141.

[87]Bancroft, *Why Does he Do That?: Inside the Minds of Angry and Controlling Men*, 76; Evans, *The Verbally Abusive Relationship: How to Recognize it and How to Respond*, 15, 109; Hirigoyen, *Stalking the Soul: Emotional Abuse and the Erosion of Identity*, 106.

[88]Bancroft, *Why Does he Do That?: Inside the Minds of Angry and Controlling Men*, 125.

way.[89] He may let her know that her understanding of what is happening and her feelings are wrong.[90] Or, he could make a derogatory comment and then claim that he was joking.[91] If she believes him, she will doubt her understanding and perceptions.[92] This further enables him to be able to control her.[93]

Fear

The victim comes to live in a state of fear. This is a result of wondering what he will be like when he comes home, when the abusive behaviour will start again, going over in her mind what she should have said and done during previous abusive incidents, and trying to figure out how to make him understand her.[94]

---

[89]Evans, *The Verbally Abusive Relationship: How to Recognize it and How to Respond*, 109.

[90]Ibid., 15.

[91]Ibid., 25.

[92]Ibid.

[93]Bancroft, *Why Does he Do That?: Inside the Minds of Angry and Controlling Men*, 50.

[94]Ellis and Powers, *The Secret of Overcoming Verbal Abuse: Getting Off the Emotional Roller Coaster and Regaining Control of Your Life*, 25.

If previous abusive incidents come to mind, she might become fearful or scared of saying or doing the wrong thing.[95] The result could be that she is anxious when she is with him.[96] She watches his facial expressions, gestures, and tone of voice in order not to upset him.[97] She could also become fearful if he tracks her time, controls who she sees, how much money she spends, how, when, and what she cooks, and what she can wear.[98] If she confronts him about his behaviour, and he becomes angry, she may become fearful of his anger.[99] If he threatens her, the children, or the family pet in some way, she will almost certainly live in fear.[100] It is likely that she will remain at home and become a recluse.[101]

---

[95]Loring, *Emotional Abuse*, 38; Evans, *The Verbally Abusive Relationship: How to Recognize it and How to Respond*, 53.

[96]Sarah Scheckter, "Emotionally Abusive Relationships," *Perelman School of Medicine, Department of Psychiatry Penn Behavioral Health* http://www.med.upenn.edu/psychotherapy/Schechter--EmotionallyAbusive.html (accessed January 8, 2014).

[97]Hirigoyen, *Stalking the Soul: Emotional Abuse and the Erosion of Identity*, 156; Miller, *No Visible Wounds: Identifying Nonphysical Abuse of Women by their Men*, 25.

[98]Stark, *Coercive Control: How Men Entrap Women in Personal Life*, 242, 257.

[99]Evans, *The Verbally Abusive Relationship: How to Recognize it and How to Respond*, 62.

[100]Ibid., 193; Miller, *No Visible Wounds: Identifying Nonphysical Abuse of Women by their Men*, 47.

[101]Stark, *Coercive Control: How Men Entrap Women in Personal Life*, 258.

Guilt

The emotional abuser may try to make the victim feel guilty.[102] This can be done by coercing the victim to do something wrong, only to say afterwards that she is a bad person for having done it.[103] Or, by claiming that not going along with him is unfair to him or that she is oppressing him by talking to him about the way that he treats her.[104] If she takes on his guilt, she becomes responsible for the relationship.[105]

Worry

The victim will start to worry. She may worry, for example, about what her husband might do to her, the children, what he says and does behind her back to others, and how he will treat her when

---

[102]Loring, *Emotional Abuse*, 43.

[103]Ibid., 43.

[104]Bancroft, *Why Does he Do That?: Inside the Minds of Angry and Controlling Men*, 125; Evans, *The Verbally Abusive Relationship: How to Recognize it and How to Respond*, 124; Hirigoyen, *Stalking the Soul: Emotional Abuse and the Erosion of Identity*, 121.

[105]Hirigoyen, *Stalking the Soul: Emotional Abuse and the Erosion of Identity*, 154.

he comes home.[106] Even though it is natural for her to worry about how he will relate to her, this kind of thinking does not prevent or stop his abusive behaviour.[107]

Inhibition

Due to living in a state of fear of displeasing her husband, and having lost trust in her thoughts and perceptions, the wife becomes inhibited. This is especially true when he engages in stalking behaviour, such as calling her throughout the day, checking her emails, reacting angrily or sulking when she spends time with friends or family, or criticizing her clothing.[108] When she is with other people, she will be concerned that she not say or do something that will trigger an angry or sulky response from him. She thus becomes inhibited when she is with other people.

---

[106]Ellis and Powers, *The Secret of Overcoming Verbal Abuse: Getting Off the Emotional Roller Coaster and Regaining Control of Your Life*, 25.

[107]Ibid., 18.

[108]Stark, *Coercive Control: How Men Entrap Women in Personal Life*, 257.

Anger

When the victim is abused, she will experience anger due to the way that he is treating her.[109] This is because she is unable to do anything to change it. With time, her anger will develop into resentment.[110] She might also be angry at herself for giving in to his treatment and at others for not doing anything about it.[111] The anger that she experiences makes her feel increased guilt about being angry and means that he gains control over her emotions.[112]

Shame

The shame that the victim experiences is because of the belief that she is bad because of something she has or has not done.[113] She thinks that there is something wrong with her and therefore does not

---

[109]Hirigoyen, *Stalking the Soul: Emotional Abuse and the Erosion of Identity*, 21.

[110]Ibid., 107.

[111]Miller, *No Visible Wounds: Identifying Nonphysical Abuse of Women by their Men*, 280.

[112]Ellis and Powers, *The Secret of Overcoming Verbal Abuse: Getting Off the Emotional Roller Coaster and Regaining Control of Your Life*, 123, 124.

[113]Nicols, "Violence Against Women: The Extent of the Problem," In *"Intimate Violence Against Women: When Spouses, Partners, or Lovers Attack*, edited by Paula Lundberg-Love and Shelly Marmion, 19.

deserve to be accepted by others.[114] She may feel shame because her husband does not love her, and for allowing him to humiliate her.[115] The shame may lead her to become passive and helpless.[116]

Changed Mental State

The emotionally abusive behaviour affects the victim's thinking. She might believe that she is as inadequate as her partner claims.[117] "Flooding" can occur, which is when flashbacks, intrusive thoughts, and/or painful memories bombard the victim's thinking.[118] This will lead to her cognitive thinking and ability to judge being negatively affected.[119] Due to the techniques he employs to confuse her, and if she allows him to define her reality, she will

---

[114]Ibid.

[115]Hirigoyen, *Stalking the Soul: Emotional Abuse and the Erosion of Identity*, 21; Miller, *No Visible Wounds: Identifying Nonphysical Abuse of Women by their Men*, 280.

[116]Engel, *The Emotionally Abused Woman: Overcoming Destructive Patterns and Reclaiming Yourself*, 31.

[117]Ellis and Powers, *The Secret of Overcoming Verbal Abuse: Getting Off the Emotional Roller Coaster and Regaining Control of Your Life*, 111.

[118]Loring, *Emotional Abuse*, 39.

[119]Ibid.

think that she is losing her mind.[120] It is likely that she will magnify his bad behaviour and then minimize that bad behaviour when he treats her better. Or, she might magnify her faults and minimize her qualities.[121]

The result is that her sense of self is adversely affected and she comes to believe that she is inadequate in some way.[122] In her daily life she could become easily distracted and preoccupied. She will have difficulty concentrating and have decreased capacity to perceive, think, and reason. It may result in her distrusting her intuition, judgment, and/or perceptions. She may become obsessive about her situation, forgetful, lose things, become accident prone, and/or engage in behaviours as an escape from her feelings, such as overeating and oversleeping.[123]

---

[120]Bancroft, *Why Does he Do That?: Inside the Minds of Angry and Controlling Men,* 67, 72; NiCarthy, *Getting Free: A Handbook for Women in Abusive Situations,* 1.

[121]Ellis and Powers, *The Secret of Overcoming Verbal Abuse: Getting Off the Emotional Roller Coaster and Regaining Control of Your Life,* 103.

[122]Rachel Novsak, Tina Mandelj, and Barbara Simonic, "Therapeutic Implications of Religious-Related Emotional Abuse," *Journal of Aggression, Maltreatment, & Trauma* Vol. 21, Issue 1 (2012): 31-44; Engel, *The Emotionally Abused Woman: Overcoming Destructive Patterns and Reclaiming Yourself,* 10; Evans, *The Verbally Abusive Relationship: How to Recognize it and How to Respond,* 53; Ellis and Powers, *The Secret of Overcoming Verbal Abuse: Getting Off the Emotional Roller Coaster and Regaining Control of Your Life,* 111.

[123]Ellis and Powers, *The Secret of Overcoming Verbal Abuse: Getting Off the Emotional Roller Coaster and Regaining Control of Your Life,* 26.

Emotional, Behavioural, and Mental Dependence upon the Abuser

The wife will gradually become less communicative in order to avoid upsetting her husband. She may even stop saying what she thinks altogether because she is scared of being called names.[124] She may do this at first because she wants to respect him, but will eventually come to do this because she is scared of his anger.[125] She may even think that there is something wrong with her as a person for wanting to share with him.[126] He might demand that she does what he says in all areas of life. Examples are cooking, finances, clothing, housework, and the children.[127] She will eventually try to anticipate what he is thinking and wanting.[128] She believes that by doing so she can prevent him from becoming angry or that she will

---

[124] NiCarthy, *Getting Free: A Handbook for Women in Abusive Situations*, 33.

[125] Ibid.

[126] Ibid.

[127] Ibid., 233.

[128] Ellis and Powers, *The Secret of Overcoming Verbal Abuse: Getting Off the Emotional Roller Coaster and Regaining Control of Your Life*, 29; Miller, *No Visible Wounds: Identifying Nonphysical Abuse of Women by their Men*, 280.

eventually be loved and accepted by him.[129] She no longer thinks that her thoughts and desires are important and becomes dependent on his thoughts about her and behaves accordingly.[130] She no longer has a sense of self and does not believe that she would be able to survive if the abuser would leave her.[131] There may be times when he gives her the emotional connection that she craves.[132] The result is that when he reverts back to being angry, she is devastated and tries to win back his love and approval.[133]

Physical Ailments

Since the mind and the body are interconnected, her thoughts in response to the abuse affect her physical condition.[134] It is claimed

---

[129]Ellis and Powers, *The Secret of Overcoming Verbal Abuse: Getting Off the Emotional Roller Coaster and Regaining Control of Your Life*, 46.

[130]NiCarthy, *Getting Free: A Handbook for Women in Abusive Situations*, 233; Ellis and Powers, *The Secret of Overcoming Verbal Abuse: Getting Off the Emotional Roller Coaster and Regaining Control of Your Life*, 112.

[131]Miller, *No Visible Wounds: Identifying Nonphysical Abuse of Women by their Men*, 32.

[132]Loring, *Emotional Abuse*, 28, 45.

[133]Ibid., 28; Ellis and Powers, *The Secret of Overcoming Verbal Abuse: Getting Off the Emotional Roller Coaster and Regaining Control of Your Life*, 46.

[134]Ellis and Powers, *The Secret of Overcoming Verbal Abuse: Getting Off the Emotional Roller Coaster and Regaining Control of Your Life*, 27.

that victims of emotional abuse characteristically suffer from headaches, respiratory problems, arthritis, bladder problems, stomach problems, sleep disturbances, weight loss or gain, back pain, palpitations, and high blood pressure.[135]

Loneliness

Trying to keep the abuser's love and acceptance, only to be confronted with recurrent abuse, leads to the wife becoming lonely.[136] The loneliness is due to a lack of relationship with her spouse and a lack of relationship with other people who understand her situation. She thinks and feels that she has no relationships with people who understand her. This experience of loneliness is exaggerated when he says that he loves her but behaves

---

[135]Ellis and Powers, *The Secret of Overcoming Verbal Abuse: Getting Off the Emotional Roller Coaster and Regaining Control of Your Life,* 28;Loring, *Emotional Abuse,* 218; Evans, *The Verbally Abusive Relationship: How to Recognize it and How to Respond,* 73; Hirigoyen, *Stalking the Soul: Emotional Abuse and the Erosion of Identity,* 155; Miller, *No Visible Wounds: Identifying Nonphysical Abuse of Women by their Men,* 44; Jerome Pieters et al., "Emotional, Physical, and Sexual Abuse: The Experiences of Men and Women," *Institute for the Equality of Men and Women,* http ://igvm-iefh.belgium.be. (Accessed November 10, 2014).
[136]Loring, *Emotional Abuse,* 25.

in an abusive way toward her.[137] When this happens, she feels that she is all alone.[138]

Depression

As well as feeling lonely in her isolated situation, the wife becomes sad.[139] This sadness leads to depression.[140] The more that she submits to the abuse, the more depressed she will become.[141] If she lives like this for any period of time, she will come to live in a constant state of depression.

---

[137]Evans, *The Verbally Abusive Relationship: How to Recognize it and How to Respond*, 195.

[138]NiCarthy, *Getting Free: A Handbook for Women in Abusive Situations*, 1.

[139]Loring, *Emotional Abuse*, 25.

[140]Evans, *The Verbally Abusive Relationship: How to Recognize it and How to Respond*, 95.

[141]Hirigoyen, *Stalking the Soul: Emotional Abuse and the Erosion of Identity*, 152;Rachel Novsak, Tina Mandelj, and Barbara Simonic, "Therapeutic Implications of Religious-Related Emotional Abuse," *Journal of Aggression, Maltreatment, & Trauma* Vol. 21, Issue 1 (2012): 31-44.

Sorrow

If the wife internalizes the abusive treatment, she will become sorrowful.[142] Her sorrow is about the marriage that she longed for and never had and for the husband who she wanted to love. This husband appeared for brief moments but just as quickly disappeared.[143]

Moving Forward With Compassion

The way that David was treating Hannah is known as emotional abuse. This is any non-physical behaviour that is designed to control, intimidate, subjugate, punish, or isolate another person resulting in the victim becoming emotionally, behaviourally, and mentally dependent on the abuser. There are a number of behaviours involved in emotional abuse. These include verbal abuse, coercion and threats, minimizing, denying, and blaming, intimidation, mind games, isolation, male privilege, financial control, using the

---

[142]Rachel Novsak, Tina Mandelj, and Barbara Simonic, "Therapeutic Implications of Religious-Related Emotional Abuse," *Journal of Aggression, Maltreatment, & Trauma* Vol. 21, Issue 1 (2012): 31-44.
[143]Miller, *No Visible Wounds: Identifying Nonphysical Abuse of Women by their Men*, 280.

children, exhibiting two personalities, jealousy, and good periods. These behaviours are used together or separately. Their cumulative effect is that the abuser gains control of the victim.

There are a number of common effects of emotional abuse on the victim. These are: confusion, doubt, fear, guilt, worry, inhibition, anger, shame, a changed mental state, emotional, behavioural, and mental dependence upon the abuser, physical ailments, loneliness, depression, and sorrow.

To be able to help the emotionally abused wife know the Lord and live in a God-honouring way in her situation, it is essential to understand what the Bible teaches about her nature as a human being, the effect of sin on the marital relationship, in what way she is renewed in Christ, and what the Bible teaches about headship and submission in marriage.

Chapter Two

Male and Female in the Image of God

In order to help a woman in an emotionally abusive marriage, it is important to first understand what the Bible teaches about who she is as a human being. To come to this understanding, this chapter will look at the origins of human life in the first chapters of Genesis in order to discover what it means for a woman to be made in the image of God and what it means that she is her husband's helper. Paul's teaching in 1 Corinthians 11:7 will be studied to see what it means that the wife is her husband's glory. The consequences of Adam and Eve's sin on the marital relationship as described in Genesis 3:16 will be examined with emphasis on how these verses are of relevance to an emotionally abusive marriage.

To understand how the woman can live as a Christian in such a marriage, the chapter will continue by looking at Christ being the image of God and what renewal of the image of God in Christ is for believers. The last section of the chapter will cover the issues of submission and headship in Christian marriage. This chapter lays a foundation to provide a biblical approach for helping women in emotionally abusive marriages and for discovering what it means for the wife to live in Christ, hereby fulfilling her purpose of glorifying him and living in her identity as a child of God.

Image of God in Genesis 1

The origins of human life are described in the first chapter of Genesis. In Genesis 1:26-28, we discover that in the beginning God deliberately chose to make human beings in his image.[144] No other aspect of creation is described as being made in his image. In these verses we read that both the male and the female are equally made in his image and both are given the mandate by God to be fruitful, multiply, and rule over creation.[145] The male and the female are both equally blessed by God and because they are equal, have the same

---

[144]Linda Belleville, "Women in Ministry: An Egalitarian Perspective." In *Two Views on Women in Ministry,* ed. James Beck and Linda Belleville (Grand Rapids: Zondervan, 2005), 97.

[145]Linda Belleville, *Women Leaders and the Church* (Grand Rapids: Baker Books, 2000), 97-99; R Wright, "God, Metaphor and Gender: Is the God of the Bible a Male Deity?" In *Discovering Biblical Equality: Complementarity Without Hierarchy,* ed. Ronald Pierce and Rebecca Groothuis (Downers Grove: Intervarsity Press, 2005), 289-290; Elaine Storkey, *Created or Constructed: The Great Gender Debate* (Carlisle: Paternoster Press, 2000), 87; Thomas Schreiner, "Women in Ministry: Another Complementarian Perspective." In *Two Views on Women in Ministry,* ed. James Beck and Linda Belleville (Grand Rapids: Zondervan, 2005), 272; D Briscoe, *The Preacher's Commentary: Genesis* (Nashville: Thomas Nelson Publishers, 1987), 29.

value and dignity.[146]

In this passage, the Hebrew word (*a.dam*) is used for both the male and the female. It is a word that describes the whole of humanity, not just the male.[147] This equality of men and women is reiterated in Genesis 5:1-2; 9:6; and James 3:9. In all of these verses we read that all human beings are created in the image of God.[148]

Genesis 1:26-28 does not explicitly state what it means to be made in the image of God. All that we read is that they were both given dominion over the earth and commanded to go forth and multiply. These are tasks that they were given to accomplish as

---

[146]Belleville, *Women Leaders and the Church*, 100; Wayne Grudem, "The Key Issues in the Manhood and Womanhood Controversy, And The Way Forward." In *Biblical Foundations for Manhood and Womanhood*, ed. Wayne Grudem (Wheaton: Crossway Books, 2002), 19; James Hurley, *Man and Women in Biblical Perspective* (Leicester: Inter-varsity Press, 2005), 31; George Knight, "The Family and the Church: How Should Biblical Manhood and Womanhood Work Out in Practice?" In *Recovering Biblical Manhood and Womanhood*, ed. John Piper and Wayne Grudem (Wheaton: Crossway Books, 1991), 353; Belleville, "Women in Ministry: An Egalitarian Perspective." In *Two Views on Women in Ministry*, 26; Elyse Fitzpatrick, *Helper by Design: God's Perfect Plan for Women in Marriage* (Chicago: Moody Publishers, 2003), 19.

[147]Belleville, *Women Leaders and the Church*, 97; Richard Hess, "Equality With and Without Innocence: Genesis 1-3." In *Discovering Biblical Equality: Complementarity Without Hierarchy*, ed. Ronald Pierce and Rebecca Groothuis (Downers Grove: Inter-varsity Press, 2005), 79; Craig Blomberg, "Women in Ministry: A Complementarian Perspective." In *Two Views on Women in Ministry*, ed. James Beck and Linda Belleville (Grand Rapids: Zondervan, 2005), 128.

[148]Wright, "God Metaphor and Gender: Is the God of the Bible a Male Deity?" In *Discovery Biblical Equality: Complementarity Without Hierarchy*, 290.

creatures made in God's image, they are not a description of what it means to be made in that image.

Ancient Near East practices can help us gain insight into a possible explanation of what this means. In the ancient Near East, statues were constructed by kings as a representation of their power and reign in far-off places of their realm. The statue represented the rule of the king in that area. An example of this is in Daniel 3:1 when King Nebuchadnezzar set up a statue of himself on the plain of Dura, in the province of Babylon. This statue represented his reign over Dura. Given this practice, we can probably understand the meaning of the man and the woman being made in the image of God in Genesis 1 to include their role as representatives of God's rulership over his creation.[149]

---

[149] Hess, "Equality Without Innocence: Genesis 1-3," In *Discovery Biblical Equality: Complementarity Without Hierarchy,* 81; Bill Arnold, *Genesis. The New Cambridge Bible Commentary* (New York: Cambridge University Press, 2009), 45; R Davidson, *Genesis 1-11. The Cambridge Bible Commentary on the New English Bible* (Cambridge University Press, 1973), 24; Clare Amos, *The Book of Genesis* (Werrington: Biddles Ltd., 2004), 11.

Image of God in Genesis 2

In Genesis 1, we read about the man and the woman being created together. In the following chapter, in Genesis 2, we read about how both the man and the woman were specifically created. The creation of the woman is described in detail in Genesis 2:18-25.

In this passage, we discover that the woman was created from a rib of the man.[150] Since she comes from the man's rib, that means that she is his flesh and bones. The woman is of the exact same substance as the man, and is therefore as fully human, and as fully in the image of God, as the man is.[151]

We read that the woman was made to be the man's helper because it was not good for the man to be alone (Genesis 2:18). When the man saw the woman, he confirmed her similarity to him when he recognized that she is "bone of my bone and flesh of my

---

[150]Wright, "God, Metaphor and Gender: Is the God of the Bible and a Male Deity?' In *Discovering Biblical Equality: Complementarity without Hierarchy,* 289.

[151]Bruce Ware, "Male and Female Complementarity and the Image of God." In *Biblical Foundations for Manhood and Womanhood,* ed. Wayne Grudem (Wheaton: Crossway Books, 2002), 83.

flesh" (Genesis 2:23).[152] The similarity is seen further because their relationship is described as one flesh (Genesis 2:24).[153] They are one flesh, one nature, of the same kind. If she was less human than the man, less in the image of God, or made of a different substance than him, they could not be described as one flesh.

The Woman as Adam's Helper

We read that the female was created to be a helper for the male (Genesis 2:18). The word "helper" in Hebrew is (*e.zerkenegdo*). This word means a help that is corresponding to the other, the male.[154] Elsewhere in the Old Testament, the Hebrew word (*e.zer*), or help, is used in relation to the help that God gives to someone in need, or of the help that one nation could give to another in a time of need. We can see this in Exodus 18:4;

---

[152]Hurley, *Men and Women in Biblical Perspective*, 1981; Belleville, *Women Leaders and the Church*, 25; Briscoe, *The Preacher's Commentary*, 129; Kenneth Matteus, *Genesis 1-11: 26. Vol 1A. An Exegetical & Theological Exposition Holy Scripture. The New American Commentary* (Nashville: B&H Publishing Group, 1996), 218.

[153]Ibid., 218.

[154]Frank Gaebelein, *The Expositor's Bible Commentary. Genesis, Exodus, Leviticus, Numbers* (Grand Rapids: Zondervan Publishing House, 1990), 38; Arnold, *Genesis. The New Cambridge Bible Commentary*, 60.

Deuteronomy 33:7, 26, 29; Psalm 20:2; 33:20; 70:5; 89:19; 115:9; 121:1; 124:8; 146:5; Isaiah 30:5; Ezekiel 12:14; Daniel 11:34, and Hosea 13:9.[155]

In the English language, the word "helper" can refer to a domestic servant or employee, that is, to an inferior who serves someone who is his or her superior.[156] This is not the meaning of the Hebrew word. Since the word "helper" is a translation from a different language and culture, it is important that the English meaning of the word, in our time and culture, is not read back into the meaning of the biblical text.[157]

As we have read, God is called Israel's helper and nations helped other nations when it was necessary in their time of need. This means that we can understand the term "helper" in the Bible to refer to the providing of strength that a person or a nation lacks in

---

[155]Belleville, *Women Leaders and the Church,* 101; Grudem, "The Key Issues in the Manhood and Womanhood Controversy, And The Way Forward," 31; Belleville, "Women in Ministry: An Egalitarian Perspective," 27; Briscoe, *The Preacher's Commentary. Genesis,* 43; Gordon Wenham, *Genesis 1-15. Word Biblical Commentary* (Waco: Word Books Publishers, 1987), 68; Kenneth Matteus, *Genesis 1-15. Word Biblical Commentary,* 214.

[156]*Oxford Concise English Dictionary of Current English* 9th ed. (New York: Oxford University Press, 1995), 631.

[157]Arnold, *Genesis. The New Cambridge Bible Commentary,* 60.

and of themselves.[158] In Genesis 2, the female corresponds to the male and provides help that the male lacks in and of himself. We cannot understand from the word "helper," or from the role of the woman as helper, that she is less of a person than, or inferior to, the male.[159] Both the male and the female are equally made in God's image.

The Woman as the Glory of the Man

The difference between the male and the female is addressed by Paul in 1 Corinthians 11:7. In this passage we read "For a man ought not to cover his head, since he is the image and glory of God, but woman is the glory of man" (ESV).

In this verse, Paul did not teach that the woman is the image of man, nor that the woman is not the image of God.[160] In 1 Corinthians 11, Paul gives two reasons why the woman is the man's

---

[158]Wenham, *Genesis 1-15. Word Biblical Commentary*, 68.

[159]Matteus, *Genesis 1-11: 26. Vol. 1A. An Exegetical & Theological Exposition of Holy Scripture. The New American Commentary*, 214.

[160]Hurley, *Man and Woman in Biblical Perspective*, 173, 206; Simon Kistemaker, *1 Corinthians. New Testament Commentary* (Grand Rapids: Zondervan Publishing House, 1994), 373.

glory. The first reason is seen in verse 8. In this verse we read that it is because she came from the man. Paul is referring back to Genesis 2:22, where we read that God created the woman from the man.[161] The second reason is seen in verse 9. The woman is the man's glory because she was created for the man. We know from Genesis 2 that she was created for the man to be his helper.

According to 1 Corinthians 11:1-16, the woman being the glory of the man is seen in how she relates to him. A woman is to relate to her husband in a way that corresponds with the way that she was designed to, that is, by giving him honour.[162] The woman was made to honour God and to honour her husband.[163] In this passage, the Corinthian wives were taught to honour their husbands by covering their heads when they prayed or prophesied.

---

[161] Schreiner, "Women in Ministry: Another Complementarian Perspective." In *Two Views on Women in Ministry,* 124.

[162] Ibid., 124; Hurley, *Man and Woman in Biblical Perspective,* 173; Richard Horsley, *1 Corinthians* (Nashville: Abingdon Press, 1998), 155.

[163] John Frame, "Men and Women in the Image of God," In *Recovering Biblical Manhood and Womanhood,* ed. John Piper and Wayne Grudem (Wheaton: Crossway Books, 1991), 230.

The Consequences of Adam and Eve's Sin on the Marriage Relationship in Genesis 3:16

There are consequences for the relationship between the husband and the wife in marriage because of the fall into sin in Genesis 3.[164] These consequences of Adam and Eve's disobedience to God's command are found in Genesis 3:16.

It is important to understand that this verse must not be taken as a mandate, nor as a command, for how husbands and wives are supposed to relate to each other. This is because it is describing the consequences of Adam and Eve's sin, it is not prescribing behaviour. Confirmation that this verse is not prescriptive for behaviour within marriage is reaffirmed in the New Testament.

Whenever the first chapters of Genesis are referred to when teaching is given in the New Testament about marriage, Genesis 1-2 are cited. These passages are Matthew 19:1-9; Ephesians 5:31; Mark 10:7-8; and 1 Corinthians 6:16. They refer back to the teaching given in Genesis 1 and 2 about the origin of people and of marriage. At no point in scripture does a New Testament author refer to Genesis 3:16

---

[164]Belleville, *Women Leaders and the Church,* 105; W. Gispen, *Commentaar op het Oude Testament: Genesis 1-11* (Kampen: J.H. Kok, 1974), 148.

as teaching regarding how Christian husbands and wives ought to relate to each other.[165]

The Hebrew word "desire" (*te.shu.qah*) used of the wife in Genesis 3:16, occurs in two other places in the Old Testament. These others verses are Genesis 4:7 and Songs of Solomon 7:10. Songs of Solomon 7:10 speaks of the man's desire for his lover. The difference between this passage and Genesis 3:16 is that the man's desire for his lover here cannot be understood to be sinful.[166] In Genesis 4:7, like Genesis 3:16, both terms "desire" and "rule over" are used. In chapter 4, the words are used regarding sin's desire for Cain and the instruction that God gives him to rule over it. The woman's desire for her husband in Genesis 3:16, could therefore refer to a longing for relationship with him or to a desire to control him. The husband's rule over his wife is a consequence of his

---

[165]Belleville, *Women Leaders and the Church,* 108; Hess, "Equality With and Without Innocence: Genesis 1-3." In *Discovering Biblical Equality: Complementarity Without Hierarchy,* 91-92.
[166]Belleville, *Women Leaders and the Church,* 105; Allen Ross, *Genesis. Cornerstone Biblical Commentary* (Carol Stream, Illinois: Tyndale House Publishers, 2008), 54.

disobedience to God and involves him trying to domineer her.[167]

This is relevant for helping women in emotionally abusive relationships. The control and dominance spoken of in Genesis 3:16 are sinful distortions of how husbands and wives should relate to each other. Tyrannical abuse of position and turning responsibility into rights is a result of the fall.[168] These attitudes and behaviours on the part of a Christian husband should be repented of because they are sinful.

Christ the Image of God

We are taught in the New Testament that Christ is the true image of God. The passages which teach this are 2 Corinthians 4:4; Colossians 1:15; Hebrews 1:3; John 1:18; John 12:45; and John

---

[167]Belleville, *Women Leaders and the Church*, 105; Cynthia Kimball, "Nature, Culture, and Gender Complementarity," In *Discovering Biblical Equality: Complementarity Without Hierarchy*, ed. Ronald Pierce and Rebecca Groothuis (Downers Grove: Inter-varsity Press, 2005), 470; Hurley, *Man and Woman in Biblical Perspective*, 219; Arnold, *Genesis. The New Cambridge Bible Commentary*, 70; Matteus, *Genesis 1-11: 26. Vol. 1A. An Exegetical & Theological Exposition of Holy Scripture*, 251; Walter Liefield, "The Nature of Authority in the New Testament," In *Discovering Biblical Equality: Complementarity Without Hierarchy*, ed. Ronald Pierce and Rebecca Groothuis (Downers Grove: Inter-varsity Press, 2005), 93.

[168]Schreiner, "Women in Ministry: Another Complementarian Perspective," In *Two Views on Women in Ministry*, 298; Grudem, "The Key Issues in the Manhood and Womanhood Controversy, And the Way Forward," In *Recovering Biblical Manhood and Womanhood*, 66.

14:9.[169] Since Christ is the true image of God, it is in him that we see a full reflection of God's character.[170]

We also discover in the New Testament that Christ renewed the image of God that was distorted by Adam. We read about this in Colossians 3:9-11; 2 Corinthians 3:18; and 1 Corinthians 15:49.[171] This renewed image of God, when spoken of in the New Testament, is moral. Examples of some of the qualities involved in the renewed image of God in believers include righteousness (Ephesians 4:24), purity (1 John 3:2, 3), love (1 John 3:10; 4:7), and forgiveness (Colossians 3:13).[172] The call to be renewed in the image of Christ, and for this to be seen in moral life, is given to both men and women

---

[169]Frame, "Men and Women in the Image of God," In *Recovering Biblical Manhood and Womanhood*, 228; Walter Brueggeman, *Genesis. A Bible Commentary for Teaching and Preaching* (Atlanta: John Knox Press, 1982), 34.

[170]Ware, "Male and Female Complementarity and the Image of God." In *Biblical Foundations for Manhood and Womanhood*, 79.

[171]Frame, "Men and Women in the Image of God," In *Recovering Biblical Manhood and Womanhood*, 228; Storkey, *Created or Constructed: The Great Gender Debate*, 290.

[172]Frame, "Men and Women in the Image of God," In *Recovering Biblical Manhood and Womanhood*, 228.

equally.[173] It is a call for all believers.

Renewal in the Image of God

The image of God that was defiled by Adam through his sin has been restored by the second Adam, Christ. This was accomplished through his perfect obedience (Romans 5:12-21).[174] Christ was obedient to God the Father to the point of death on a cross. The death that Christ died on the cross paid the penalty for Adam's sin. As a result, anyone who trusts Christ has died with him, and therefore no longer has to answer for sin.[175] All believers are thus

---

[173] Wright, "God, Metaphor and Gender. Is the God of the Bible a Male Deity?" In *Discovering Biblical Equality: Complementarity Without Hierarchy*, 229; Rebecca Groothuis, "Equal in Being, Unequal in Role: Exploring the Logic of Women's Subordination," In *Discovering Biblical Equality: Complementarity Without Hierarchy*, ed. Ronald Pierce and Rebecca Groothuis (Downers Grove: Inter-varsity Press, 2005), 311; Judith Balswick and Jack Balswick, "Marriage as a Partnership of Equals," In *Discovering Biblical Equality: Complementarity Without Hierarchy*, ed. Ronald Pierce and Rebecca Groothuis(Downers Grove: Inter-varsity Press, 2005), 452; Welch, *When People are Big and God is Small: Overcoming Peer Pressure, Codependency, and the Fear of Man,* 158.

[174] Paul Achtemeier, *Romans. Interpretation. A Bible Commentary for Teaching and Preaching* (Louisville: John Knox Press, 1985), 97; Grant Osbourne, ed. *Romans. The I.V.P. New Testament Commentary Series* (Downers Grove: Intervarsity Press, 2004), 141.

[175] Achtemeier, *Romans. Interpretation. A Bible Commentary for Teaching and Preaching,* 104; Grant Osbourne, ed. *Romans. The I.V.P. New Testament Commentary Series* (Downers Grove: Intervarsity Press, 2004), 150.

dead to the power of sin (Romans 6:6).[176]

Having died to sin and been raised to life in Christ, the believer is to live for righteousness (Romans 6:12-14). This is true for all believers, male and female. Every believer approaches God through Christ alone and has access to God through him alone.[177] The Holy Spirit is given to all believers (Acts 2:17-18) and all receive spiritual gifts from him (1 Corinthians 12:7, 11;1 Peter 4:10).[178] All believers are made righteous, or justified, through Christ and are called sons of God (Galatians 3:26).[179]

---

[176]Kenneth Matteus, *Genesis 1-11:26. Vol. 1A. An Exegetical & Theological Exposition of Holy Scripture. The New American Commentary*, 104; Robert Mounce, *Romans. The New American Commentary. An Exegetical and Theological Exposition of Holy Scripture* (Nashville: Broadman and Holman Publishers, 1995), 149; Grant Osbourne, ed. *Romans. The I.V.P. New Testament Commentary Series* (Downers Grove: Intervarsity Press, 2004), 154.

[177]Rebecca Groothuis, "Equal in Being, Unequal in Role: Exploring the Logic of Women's Subordination," In *Discovering Biblical Equality: Complementarity Without Hierarchy*, ed. Ronald Pierce and Rebecca Groothuis (Downers Grove: Inter-varsity Press, 2005), 311-313; Knight, "The Family and the Church: How Should Biblical Manhood and Womanhood Work Out in Practice?" in *Recovering Biblical Manhood and Womanhood*, 353; Schreiner, "Women in Ministry: Another Complementarian Perspective," In *Two Views on Women in Ministry*, 274; John Stott, *The Message of Galatians. The Bible Speaks Today* (Leicester: Inter-Varsity Press, 1968), 99.

[178]Grudem, "The Key Issues In the Manhood and Womanhood Controversy, And the way Forward," In *Biblical Foundations for Manhood and Womanhood*, 21; John MacArthur, *Galatians* (Chicago: The Moody Press, 1987), 100).

[179]Liefield, "The Nature of Authority in the New Testament," In *Discovering Biblical Equality: Complementarity Without Hierarchy*, 152; Philip Ryken, *Galatians. Reformed Expository Commentary* (Phillipsburg: P&R Publishing, 2005), 142; Mounce, *Romans. The New American Commentary. An Exegetical and Theological Exposition of Holy Scripture*, 132.

Having been renewed in Christ, believers are called to become like him, who is the image of God (Colossians 1:15; 3:9-11; 2 Corinthians 3:18; 4:4).[180] Every believer is called to be full of the Holy Spirit, to demonstrate the fruit of the Spirit (Ephesians 5:18; Galatians 5:22), to focus on the things above (Colossians 3:1-4), and to live according to the moral qualities of the new person in Christ (Colossians 3:12-17; Ephesians 4:17-32).[181]

This means that a woman who is being emotionally abused by her husband has access to God through Christ, has the Holy Spirit indwelling her, has been given spiritual gifts, is called to become like Christ in her character, and is personally responsible for doing so. She has access to all the blessings in Christ (2 Peter 1:3, 4). This is her calling in life. Her husband cannot prevent her from living for Christ, nor should she place pleasing him above her calling to honour Christ.

---

[180] Wright, "God, Metaphor and Gender. Is the God of the Bible a Male Deity?" In *Discovering Biblical Equality. Complementarity Without Hierarchy*, 290; Matteus, *Genesis 1-11:26. Vol. 1A. An Exegetical & Theological Exposition of Holy Scripture. The New American Commentary*, 171; Osbourne, ed. *Romans. The I.V.P. New Testament Commentary Series*, 153.

[181] Robert Wall, *Colossians and Philemon. The IVP New Testament Commentary Series* (Downers Grove: Intervarsity Press, 1993), 61; Osbourne, ed. *Romans. The I.V.P. New Testament Commentary Series*, 151.

As her husband's helper, she is to help him be God's image bearer. This means that she is to help him to become Christ-like. She is not being an appropriate helper if she allows him to control her, as by doing so he would be sinning against her.[182] She is responsible to God for her thoughts and behaviour and should never give the responsibility for her thoughts and behaviour to someone else. She is also going against her calling to be his helper if she responds to anger or jealousy toward her without question, as these are sins of the flesh (1 Corinthians 3:3; Colossians 3:8). If she does, she is inadvertently letting her husband emotionally abuse her. That is, she is allowing him to relate to her in certain non-physical ways in order to have control over her emotions, behaviour, and thoughts. By doing so, she is unwittingly enabling him to live in what is of the old nature and thereby not helping him to become a Christ-like person, which is his calling in life.[183]

We can conclude that she is not living to the glory of Christ, which is her purpose in life, if she gives in to emotional abuse.

---

[182]Laura Hendrickson, "Counseling Victims of Spousal Abuse," *Institute for Biblical Counseling & Discipleship,* mp3, http://www.ibcd.org/resources/messages/counseling-victims-of-spousal-abuse/ (accessed January 16 2014).

[183] Fitzpatrick, *Helper By Design: God's Perfect Plan for Women In Marriage,* 75.

Therefore a Christian wife should do all that she can to prevent her husband treating her in an emotionally abusive way. "Christ…is the primary relationship in the life of a Christian, and no submission to any human being can be allowed to transgress that relationship. Thus submission to another person should not require something that is incompatible with what Jesus requires."[184]

In a marital relationship, both the husband and the wife are to fulfil their responsibilities to each other.[185] Husbands are to express their headship by loving their wives and wives are to be submissive to their husbands (Colossians 3:18, 19; Ephesians 5:22-33). All other duties that are involved in the marital relationship are for the husband and wife equally.[186] Paul does not teach husbands to rule their wives, rather they are to love them as Christ loved the

---

[184]Peter Davids, *Ephesians, Philippians, Colossians, 1-2 Thessalonians, Philemon. Cornerstone Biblical Commentary*, ed. Philip Comfort (Carol Stream: Tyndale House Publishers, 2008), 291.

[185]Belleville, *Women Leaders and the Church*, 104; Thomas Schreiner, "Women in Ministry: Another Complementarian Perspective," In *Two Views on Women in Ministry*, 303; Wall, *Colossians and Philemon. The IVP New Testament Commentary Series*, 232.

[186]Belleville, *Women Leaders and the Church*, 114.

church.[187]

As has been seen, the effects of the fall in Genesis 3:16 are never used as normative teaching for marriage, Genesis 1:27 and 2:23-24 are the passages that are used.[188] If a husband uses his authority to make his wife do what he wants, he is using his power and authority in a wrong way.[189] It is opposed to Jesus' teaching to his disciples when he taught them to be servant-like rather than authoritarian and domineering (Matthew 20:25-28; Mark 10:42-45; Luke 22:25-26).

Submission

Meaning of the Word

In the New Testament, wives are instructed to submit to their husbands (Ephesians 5:22; Colossians 3:18-19; 1 Peter 3:1-7). The

---

[187] I. Marshall, "Mutual Love and Submission in Marriage. Colossians 3:18-19 and Ephesians 5:21-33," In *Discovering Biblical Equality: Complementarity Without Hierarchy*, ed. Ronald Pierce and Rebecca Groothuis (Downers Grove: Inter-varsity Press, 2005), 187.

[188] Belleville, "Women in Ministry: An Egalitarian Perspective," In *Two Views on Women in Ministry*, 32.

[189] Marshall, "Mutual Love and Submission in Marriage. Colossians 3:18-19 and Ephesians 5:21-33," In *Discovering Biblical Equality: Complementarity Without Hierarchy*, 202.

word translated as "submission" is the Greek word (*hupotassō*), which means to be subject, to be subordinate.[190] The decision to submit is a voluntary act by the person themselves.[191] It is not something that can be forced on someone by the authority figure to whom they have to be submissive.

The Nature of Submission

Ephesians 5:22 teaches that the wife is to submit to her husband as to the Lord. Similar teaching is found in Colossians 3:18. In this verse in Colossians, the wife's submission is to be as is fitting in the Lord. The motive for the wife's submission is obedience to the Lord.[192] Since the manner of submission is such that it is to be pleasing to Christ, Christian submission cannot be done for personal

---

[190]Hurley, *Man and Woman in Biblical Perspective*, 142; George Knight, "Husbands and Wives as Analogies of Christ and the Church. Ephesians 5:21-33 and Colossians 3:18-19," In *Recovering Biblical Manhood and Womanhood*, ed. John Piper and Wayne Grudem (Wheaton: Crossway Books, 1991), 162; Peter O'Brien, *Colossians, Philemon. Word Biblical Commentary* (Waco: Word Books, 1982), 221; Fitzpatrick, *Helper By Design: God's Perfect Plan for Women in Marriage*, 151.

[191]Belleville, *Women Leaders and the Church*, 118; Knight, "Husbands and Wives as Analogies of Christ and the Church. Ephesians 5:21-33 and Colossians 3:18-19. In *Recovering Biblical Manhood and Womanhood*, 162; Pryde and Needham, *A Biblical Perspective of What to Do When You Are Abused By Your Husband*, 22.

[192]Fitzpatrick, *Helper By Design: God's Perfect Plan for Women in Marriage*, 152.

sinful reasons nor due to sin on the part of the husband. Neither of these correspond with what would be considered to be fitting to the Lord.[193]

We read further in Ephesians 5:23-24 that since the husband is the head of the wife, she is to submit to him in everything, as the church submits to Christ. The term "in everything" expresses the comprehensiveness of the wife's submission. Her submission is to cover all areas of her life.[194] It is not instruction on Paul's part to give into her husband's wishes about everything that he asks of her.

Peter instructs wives to be submissive to their husbands, even if the husband is not obedient to the Word (1 Peter 3:1-6). By doing

---

[193]Groothuis. "Equal in Being, Unequal in Role: Exploring the Logic of Women's Subordination." In *Discovering Biblical Equality: Complementarity Without Hierarchy,* 213; Werner Neuer, *Man & Woman in Christian Perspective* (London: Hodder & Stoughton, 1990), 125; James Bordwine, *The Pauline Doctrine of Male Headship: The Apostle versus Biblical Feminists* (Greenville: Greenville Seminary Press, 1996), 120; John Piper, "An Overview of Critical Concerns: Questions and Answers," In *Recovering Biblical Manhood and Womanhood,* ed. John Piper and Wayne Grudem (Wheaton: Crossway Books, 1991), 56; Knight, "Husbands and Wives as Analogies of the Church: Ephesians 5:21-33 and Colossians 3:18-19," In *Recovering Biblical Manhood and Womanhood,* 162; Wall, *Colossians and Philemon: The IVP New Testament Commentary Series,* 157; Peter O'Brien, *The Letter to the Ephesians. Pillar The New Testament Commentary* (Leicester: Apollos, 1999), 412.

[194]Groothuis, "Equal in Being, Unequal in Role: Exploring the Logic of Woman's Subordination," In *Discovering Biblical Equality: Complementarity Without Hierarchy,* 313; Knight, "Husbands and Wives as Analogies of the Church: Ephesians 5:21-33 and Colossians 3:18-19," In *Recovering Biblical Manhood and Womanhood,* 161, 165; O'Brien, *The Letter to the Ephesians,* 412, 417.

so, her behaviour is a witness to him.[195] In the culture at the time when Peter wrote this epistle, women were expected to follow the religion of their fathers, or after marriage, of their husbands. The fact that a Christian wife was not following the religion of her husband would be seen as rebellion against her husband's authority by the society around her.[196] This shows that a wife is to follow the Lord above other people around her and that she is to do this while leading a holy life. By being submissive to her husband in her day-to-day life, she shows appropriate respect to her non-believing husband.[197] Even though following a different religion than her husband would be seen as disrespectful, her behaviour toward him should demonstrate that she does give him appropriate respect.

Wrong Ideas Regarding Submission

Since submission is a voluntary subjection to an authority

---

[195]Belleville, *Women Leaders and the Church*, 119.

[196]Peter Davids, "A Silent Witness in Marriage: 1 Peter 3:1-7," In *Discovering Biblical Equality: Complementarity Without Hierarchy*, ed. Ronald Pierce and Rebecca Groothuis (Downers Grove: Inter-varsity Press, 2005), 226; Blomberg, "Women in Ministry: A Complementarian Perspective," In *Two Views on Women in Ministry*, 176.

[197]Belleville, *Women Leaders and the Church*, 199; Hurley, *Man and Woman in Biblical Perspective*, 154.

above a person, it does not mean that the wife is no longer to think in a critical way.[198] She is responsible before the Lord for her mind. As her husband's helper, she should continue to think biblically. By doing so, she will be able to help him in a way that is honouring to the Lord by being able to encourage him to be a person whose character corresponds to what the Bible teaches.[199]

The submission of the wife to the husband should not be absolute, nor should she submit to sin.[200] It does not mean that the wife is to subject her whole self to her husband, that she allows "slavery or tyrannical authority," nor that she allows the breaking of her will.[201] Neither should submission be used as the basis on which

---

[198]Belleville, *Women Leaders and the Church,* 118; Knight, "Husbands and Wives as Analogies of Christ and the Church: Ephesians 5:21-33 and Colossians 3:18-19," In *Recovering Biblical Manhood and Womanhood,* 162; O'Brien, *The Letter to the Ephesians. The Pillar New Testament Commentary,* 418; Fitzpatrick, *Helper By Design: God's Perfect Plan for Women in Marriage,* 96.

[199]Neuer, *Man & Woman in Christian Perspective,* 125.

[200]William Hendrikson, *New Testament Commentary: Exposition of Colossians and Philemon* (Grand Rapids: Baker Book House, 1975), 169; John Piper, "A Vision of Biblical Complementarity: Manhood and Womanhood Defined According to the Bible," In *Recovering Biblical Manhood and Womanhood,* ed. John Piper and Wayne Grudem (Wheaton: Crossway Books, 1991), 37; Piper, "An Overview of Critical Concerns: Questions and Answers," In *Recovering Biblical Manhood and Womanhood,* 56; Fitzpatrick, *Helper by Design: God's Perfect Plan for Women in Marriage,* 148.

[201]Tom Westwood, *Colossians* (Redlands: Bible Treasury Hour Inc., 1970), 104; Wall, *Colossians and Philemon. The IVP New Testament Commentary Series,* 153; O'Brien, *The Letter to the Ephesians. The Pillar New Testament Commentary,* 411; Pryde and Needham, *A Biblical Perspective of What to Do When You Are Abused By Your Husband,* 27.

the rest of her behaviour is based.[202] Her first calling is to glorify the Lord in her thinking and behaviour. From this first calling, she is then submissive to her husband. She is not to be first submissive to her husband and then function from that basis. Examples of people who refused to submit to sinful instructions of authorities above them are the Hebrew midwives (Exodus 1:17); Esther regarding Xerxes (Esther 4:16); Shadrach, Meshach, and Abednego (Daniel 3:13-18); Daniel (Daniel 6:10-14); the apostles (Acts 4:18-20; 5:27-29); and Moses' parents (Hebrews 11:23). Sapphira was submissive to her husband in Acts 5:1-11 by telling the same lie that he told to the other believers. Even though she was following an authority above her, she was held personally accountable for telling a lie and was punished by death in the same way as her husband was.[203] Both Ananias and Sapphira were held individually responsible for their own behaviour and received the same judgment and punishment for lying to the Holy Spirit.

When Peter uses Sarah's submission as an example for

---

[202] O'Brien, *The Letter to the Ephesians. The Pillar New Testament Commentary*, 418.

[203] Blomberg, "Women in Ministry: A Complementarian Perspective," In *Two Views on Women in Ministry*, 146.

Christian wives to follow, he cannot be referring to the times when she lied as instructed by her husband (Genesis 12:10-20; 20:1-7). This is because Peter instructs wives to do good. Submitting to sin would mean that the wife was being complicit in doing evil, as in the case of Sapphira, rather than doing good.

Christ the Ultimate Authority

Since a wife's submission to her husband is to be as is fitting in the Lord (Colossians 3:18), this presupposes that she is already submitted to Christ. Christ is to be the ultimate authority in her life, not her husband.[204] As has been seen, Sapphira was held personally accountable and punished for her words before the Lord (Acts 5:1-11). Her husband's authority did not replace her own individual responsibility to obey the Lord.

---

[204]Neuer, *Man & Woman in Christian Perspective*, 125; Piper, "A Vision of Biblical Complementarity: Manhood and Womanhood Defined According to the Bible," In *Recovering Biblical Manhood and Womanhood*, 31, 37; Piper, "An Overview of Critical Concerns: Questions and Answers," In *Recovering Biblical Manhood and Womanhood*, 57; David Hay, *Colossians* (Nashville: Abingdon Press, 2000), 143; Pryde and Needham, *A Biblical Perspective of What to Do When You Are Abused By Your Husband*, 11, 27; Fitzpatrick, *Helper By Design: God's Perfect Plan for Women in Marriage*, 150.

Headship

Meaning of the Word

Paul teaches in Ephesians 5:23 that husbands are the head of their wives. The Greek word that is translated as head is (*kephalē*).[205] It is assumed in this book that the husband being the head of his wife means that he has a position of authority over her.

The Responsibility to Love

There are three passages in the New Testament which speak about how a husband should treat his wife. These passages are 1 Peter 3:7; Ephesians 5:25-33; and Colossians 3:19. All three of these passages teach the importance of the loving care that the husband is to provide for his wife.

In 1 Peter 3:7, Peter instructs husbands to live with their wives in an understanding way, which involves showing honour to her as the weaker partner. Both Ephesians 5:25-33 and Colossians

---

[205]Hurley, *Man & Woman in Biblical Perspective,* 144.

3:19 instruct husbands to love their wives.[206] Colossians adds that husbands are not to be harsh with them.

Paul elaborates on the kind of love the husband is to give his wife in Ephesians 5:25-33. He is to sacrificially give of himself to her, nourishing and cherishing her, for her good.[207] His love should be like the love that Christ has for the church.[208]

In Ephesians, Paul commands husbands to love their wives as their own bodies.[209] The wife is said to be part of his body as the church is the body of Christ. When the husband loves his wife, he is

---

[206]Knight, "Husbands and Wives as Analogies of Christ and the Church: Ephesians 5:21-33 and Colossians 3:18-19," In *Recovering Biblical Manhood and Womanhood,* 166; Schreiner, "Women in Ministry: Another Complementarian Perspective," In *Two Views on Women in Ministry,* 298.

[207]Knight, "Husbands and Wives as Analogies of Christ and the Church: Ephesians 5:21-33 and Colossians 3:18-19," In *Recovering Biblical Manhood and Womanhood,* 168; Knight, "The Family and the Church: How Should Biblical Manhood and Womanhood Work Out in Practice?" In *Recovering Biblical Manhood and Womanhood,* 353; F. F. Bruce, *The Epistle to the Ephesians* (London: Pickering &Inglis, Ltd., 1961), 115; O'Brien, *The Letter to the Ephesians. The Pillar New Testament Commentary,* 419.

[208]Groothuis, "Equal in Being, Unequal in Role: Exploring the Logic of Woman's Subordination," In *Discovering Biblical Equality,* 313; Hendrickson, "Counseling Victims of Spousal Abuse," *Institute for Biblical Counseling & Discipleship,* mp3.

[209]Aida Spencer, "Jesus' Treatment of Women in the Gospels," In *Discovering Biblical Equality: Complementarity Without Hierarchy,* ed. Ronald Pierce and Rebecca Groothuis (Downers Grove: Inter-varsity Press, 2005), 199.

also loving himself.[210] This connection between a husband and a wife is because they are no longer two, but one flesh (v.31). Since the husband is one flesh with his wife, it is in his own best interest to care for her.[211]

The Responsibility to Imitate Christ

Paul teaches in Ephesians 5:25 that husbands are to imitate Christ in the manner in which they love their wives.[212] Christ loved others by serving and dying for them (John 13:1-17; 1 John 3:16).[213] If the husband has Christ-like love for his wife, he will have the

---

[210]Piper, "A Vision of Biblical Complementarity: Manhood and Womanhood Defined According to the Bible," In *Recovering Biblical Manhood and Womanhood*, 31; Arthur Patzia, *Ephesians, Colossians, Philemon. New International Biblical Commentary* (Peabody: Hendrickson, 1990), 272.

[211]F.F. Bruce, *The Epistle to the Colossians to Philemon and to the Ephesians* (Grand Rapids: Wm. Eerdmans Publishing Co., 1984), 391.

[212]Hurley, *Man and Woman in Biblical Perspective*, 147; Bordwine, *The Pauline Doctrine of Male Headship. The Apostle versus Biblical Feminists*, 140; Raymond Ortland, "Male-Female Equality and Headship: Genesis 1-3," In *Recovering Biblical Manhood and Womanhood*, ed. John Piper and Wayne Grudem, (Wheaton: Crossway Books, 1991), 86; Knight, "Husbands and Wives as Analogies of Christ and the Church: Ephesians 5:21-33 and Colossians 3:18-19," In *Recovering Biblical Manhood and Womanhood*, 166.

[213]Neuer, *Man & Woman in Christian Perspective*, 124.

good of his wife as his objective.[214] Since a husband's headship is to imitate Christ's love for others, the assertive, crushing behaviour involved in emotional abuse should have no place in how a Christian husband relates to his wife.[215]

Headship is Not Ruling Forcefully

Husbands are not taught to have authority over their wives, nor to ensure that their wives submit to them.[216] The authority that husbands have is derived from God and should therefore be

---

[214]Piper, "An Overview of Critical Concerns: Questions and Answers," In *Recovering Biblical Manhood and Womanhood*, 56; Knight, "Husbands and Wives as Analogies of Christ and the Church: Ephesians 5:21-33 and Colossians 3:18-19," In *Recovering Biblical Manhood and Womanhood*, 166; Craig Blomberg, *1 Corinthians. The NIV Application Commentary* (Grand Rapids: Zondervan Publishing House, 1994), 217; Linda Mercadante, *From Hierarchy to Equality: A Comparison of Past and Present Interpretations of 1 Corinthians 11:2-16 in Relation to the Changing Status of Women in Society* (Vancouver: Regent College, 1978), 166.

[215]John Stott, *The Message of 1 Timothy & Titus: The Bible Speaks Today* (Leicester: Inter-varsity Press, 1996), 80.

[216]Hurley, *Man and Woman in Biblical Perspective*, 147; O'Brien, *The Letter to the Ephesians. The Pillar New Testament Commentary*, 419; Henry Uprichard, *Ephesians. An EP Commentary* (Auburn: Evangelical Press, 2004), 311; Piper, "A Vision of Biblical Complementarity: Manhood and Womanhood Defined According to the Bible," In *Recovering Biblical Manhood and Womanhood*, 32; Roger Nicole, "Biblical Hermeneutics: Basic Principles and Questions of Gender," In *Discovering Biblical Equality: Complementarity Without Hierarchy*, ed. Ronald Pierce and Rebecca Groothuis (Downers Grove: Inter-varsity Press, 2005), 358; Pryde and Needham, *A Biblical Perspective of What to Do When You Are Abused By Your Husband*, 33.

practiced in a way that is subject to scripture and honours God.[217] Jesus taught his disciples that the use of authority that honours him is that of being a servant. He forbade his disciples from ruling over others.[218]

We can therefore conclude that for a husband to relate to his wife in order to have power over her is wrong.[219] He cannot forbid his wife things that the Bible commands, as this would mean that he would be going against the teaching of scripture. This means that he cannot forbid her from reading her Bible, having fellowship with others, attending church, or thinking in a biblical way.[220] Supervising details of her life is not headship as the Lord intends, nor is self-centeredness or self-assertion.[221]

---

[217] Hurley, *Man and Woman in Biblical Perspective*, 150.

[218] Ibid., 148; Blomberg, "Women in Ministry: A Complementarian Perspective," In *Two Views on Women in Ministry*, 160; Wm. Goode, "Wife Abuse (90)," *National Association of Nouthetic Counselors*, Annual Conference, 1990, CD N9027.

[219] Marshall, "Mutual Love and Submission in Marriage: Colossians 3:18-19 and Ephesians 5:21-33," In *Discovering Biblical Equality: Complementarity Without Hierarchy*, 202.

[220] Bordwine, *The Pauline Doctrine of Male Headship. The Apostle versus Biblical Feminists*, 147; Fitzpatrick, *Helper By Design: God's Perfect Plan for Women in Marriage*, 148.

[221] Piper, "A Vision of Biblical Complementarity: Manhood and Womanhood Defined According to the Bible," In *Recovering Biblical Manhood and Womanhood*, 310; Schreiner, "Women in Ministry: Another Complementarian Perspective," In *Two Views on Women in Ministry*, 298; Patzia, *Ephesians, Colossians, 1-2 Thessalonians, Philemon. Cornerstone Biblical Commentary*, 269.

The Riches of God's Intention for Humanity

Men and women were made deliberately by God to reflect himself and his rulership over creation. The woman was created from the man to be his helper and glory. The fact that God made the woman from the man means that she is of the same substance as him. As his helper, she can provide strength that he lacks in himself and is to help him reflect the image of God. This relationship between the husband and wife was marred by the fall into sin. The consequences of Adam and Eve's sin is that there is a power struggle in relationships. Christ's death and resurrection have renewed the image of God in men and women that was marred by sin. Being dead to sin and alive to righteousness, both men and women are called to reflect Christ in their characters. In a Christian marriage, this means that both the husband and the wife are responsible for their own individual obedience to Christ. He is the ultimate authority for them both. The wife is to submit to her husband out of love and obedience to Christ. This submission is a voluntary choice on her part. While having an attitude of submission to and respect toward her husband in all areas of her life, she should not submit to sin, be complicit in it, tolerate her husband treating her in a sinful way, nor allow him to control her thinking or behaviour. The husband is called to love his wife, as Christ loved the church, seeing her as his own body, and respecting her as the weaker vessel. He is not to exercise dominion over her, but is to serve and love her as Christ does the church.

Chapter Three

This chapter will build on the teaching of the previous chapter. In chapter two, we saw that a wife is made in the image of God and is the helper and glory of her husband to help him to reflect the character of Christ. Her first calling is to glorify Christ in her own life. Being her husband's helper flows out of her relationship with God and is subject to it. This chapter will provide a biblical approach for helping women in emotionally abusive marriages and will discover what it means for the wife to live in Christ, hereby fulfilling her purpose of glorifying him and living in her identity as a child of God. It will explain what it means to have the glory of Christ as her purpose in life and her identity in him. Given the difficulty of reconciling the command of God to be submissive to her husband when she knows that to do so in an emotionally abusive marriage will lead to him having more control over her, an approach will be suggested about how to deal with this issue. Since living to the glory of Christ involves dealing with her heart, the meaning of the heart will be explained, as well as what heart change is. From this understanding, biblical solutions to a number of heart issues will be suggested. These are confusion and doubt, worry, fear, guilt, anger, shame, loneliness, and depression. Following on from this, an approach to honoring Christ in her home will be suggested. Lastly, the importance of the church for the wife will be explained.

Purpose in Life is to Glorify Christ

Paul goes to great lengths to teach us in Romans that all believers are called to live for righteousness (Romans 6:12-14). Regardless of a believer's circumstances, his or her purpose in life is to live for the glory of Christ. A woman who is in an emotionally abusive marriage is therefore called to live for this purpose. She has been saved from alienation and hostility in her mind to be holy and blameless before God (Colossians 1:21, 22), is chosen to be holy and blameless before him (Ephesians 1:4), is to be conformed to the image of God's son (Romans 8:29), and is called to obey the Lord (1 Peter 1:2).

The Identity of the Wife is in Christ

All believers are renewed in Christ and are called to live for his glory. Their identity is in him. This means that the identity of the Christian woman in an emotionally abusive relationship is in Christ. Her identity in him includes being blessed in Christ with every spiritual blessing in the heavenly places (Ephesians 1:3), chosen before the foundation of the world to be holy and blameless (Ephesians 1:4), predestined for adoption (Ephesians 1:5), redeemed through his blood and forgiven of sin (Ephesians 1:7), the recipient of an inheritance (Ephesians 1:11), predestined to be to the praise of his glory (Ephesians 1:11), sealed with the Holy Spirit as a guarantee of the inheritance (Ephesians 1:13, 14), and being filled in him (Colossians 2:10).

A woman in an emotionally abusive relationship is to live according to her purpose, which is to glorify Christ, and is to find her identity in him. It is from this purpose and identity in Christ that she is to relate to her abusive husband.

Submission in an Emotionally Abusive Relationship

Wives are instructed in scripture to be submissive to their husbands in a way that is fitting in the Lord (Ephesians 5:22; Colossians 3:18-19; 1 Peter 3:1-7). As has been seen, the word translated as "submission" is the Greek word (*hupotassō*), which means to be subject, to be subordinate.[222] Submission is a voluntary act by the person themselves and cannot be forced upon someone.[223]

Since submission has to be such that it is fitting in the Lord, it assumes that she is already submissive to the Lord in the first place. It is from this submission to the Lord that she is submissive to her husband. Since scripture never contradicts scripture, submission to her husband cannot involve submission to sin nor to her being prevented from living according to her purpose of glorifying

---

[222]Hurley, *Man and Woman in Biblical Perspective*, 142; Knight, "Husbands and Wives as Analogies of Christ and the Church: Ephesians 5:21-33 and Colossians 3:18-19," In *Recovering Biblical Manhood and Womanhood*, 162; O'Brien, *Colossians, Philemon. Word Biblical Commentary*, 221; Fitzpatrick, *Helper by Design: God's Perfect Plan for Women in Marriage*, 151.

[223]Belleville, *Women Leaders and the Church*, 118; Knight, "Husbands and Wives as Analogies of Christ and the Church: Ephesians 5:21-33 and Colossians 3:18-19," In *Recovering Biblical Manhood and Womanhood*, 162; Pryde and Needham, *A Biblical Perspective of What to Do When You Are Abused By Your Husband*, 22.

Christ.[224]

The wife is responsible and accountable to God for her thoughts and behaviour. She should never give this responsibility to another person by allowing that other person to control her. In an emotionally abusive relationship, the husband uses things such as fear, guilt, shame, insinuations, and accusations in order to have control over his wife. If she yields to him when he treats her in these ways, it will result in her living in fear, guilt, shame, and to believing falsehoods about herself. These heart issues belong to the old nature. This means that if she yields to him, she will be living in what belongs to the old nature, from which Christ has redeemed her, instead of living in the new person that she is in Christ. We can conclude that if she yields to, or is submissive to emotional abuse, she will be living in what belongs to the old nature. Since Christ has redeemed her from the old nature, and called her to live in him, the

---

[224]Groothuis, "Equal in Being, Unequal in Role: Exploring the Logic of Woman's Subordination," In *Discovering Biblical Equality: Complementarity Without Hierarchy*, 313; Neuer, *Man & Woman in Christian Perspective*, 125; Bordwine, *The Pauline Doctrine of Male Headship. The Apostle versus Biblical Feminists*, 120; Piper, "An Overview of Critical Concerns: Questions and Answers," In *Recovering Biblical Manhood and Womanhood*, 56; Knight, "Husbands and Wives as Analogies of Christ and the Church: Ephesians 5:21-33 and Colossians 3:18-19," In *Recovering Biblical Manhood and Womanhood*, 162; Wall, *Colossians and Philemon. The IVP New Testament Commentary Series*, 157; O'Brien, *The Letter to the Ephesians. The Pillar New Testament Commentary*, 412.

wife cannot go along with emotionally abusive behaviour. Otherwise she is going against the purpose of Christ for her life and is bringing herself back into what he has saved her from by his work on the cross.

In addition to this, if she goes along with behaviours such as anger, (veiled) threats, jealousy, and punishments when relating to her, she is thereby inadvertently enabling him to live in what belongs to the old nature. In so doing, she is not fulfilling her role as his God-given helper who is called to help him reflect the character of God. It is important that she does not take upon herself the responsibility to ensure that he is happy, not angry, or not jealous. The reason for this is because his thoughts, emotions, and behaviour are his responsibility before God for which he will have to give account.

Often in emotionally abusive relationships, the husband uses control in areas that are not explicitly taught about in scripture. For example, he may demand that she answer the phone on the third ring, answer an email within five minutes after he has sent it, or scrutinize how she uses the minutes of her day. Wisdom is needed to know how to respond in such situations. The wife should ask "If I do this, where will it lead to, what will it result in?" For example, if it leads to him controlling her by not allowing her to go out the house, it is probably wise that she refrain from complying. The reason for this is because she will not be fulfilling her responsibilities to others to be a blessing to them, nor will she be able to be the person she should be toward the rest of the family. If she would yield to such attempts to control, she will compound the problem because she is putting herself in a position of living in what is of the old nature and is inadvertently enabling him to do the same.

Heart Issues

What the Heart Is

The Bible uses different Greek words interchangeably for the inner person. These include "heart" *(kardia* - Matthew 19:8*),* "mind," *(dianonia*– Matthew 22:37*, phrenes*– Romans 8:6*,* and *nous* – Luke 24:45*),* "soul," *(psuche*– Matthew 11:29*),* "conscience" *(suneidesis*– 2 Corinthians 1:12*),* "inner self" (1 Peter

3:4), and "inner man" (2 Corinthians 4:16).[225] We will summarize these references for the inner person by using the word "heart."

The word "heart" refers to the core of a person, that is, to his or her character. It is the non-physical part of what it means to be human.[226] The heart of a person is where his or her thoughts, will, speech, and attitudes originate.[227] It is our moral centre and where we decide whether or not we will live for God, whom we will worship, and whom we will love.[228]

What Heart Change Is

Whatever is going on in a person's heart determines how that person will function.[229] Jesus teaches in Mark 7:21-23 that it is

---

[225]Edward Welch, *Blame it on the Brain: Distinguishing Chemical Imbalances, Brain Disorders, and Disobedience* (Phillipsburg: P&R Publishing, 1998), 35.

[226] Leland Ryken, James Wilhoit, and Tremper Longman, ed. *Dictionary of Biblical Imagery: An encyclopedic exploration of the images, symbols, motifs, metaphors, figures of speech and literary patterns of the Bible* (Downers Grove: InterVarsity Press, 1998), 368.

[227]Ibid., 36; Howard Eyrich and William Hines, *Curing the Heart: A Model for Biblical Counseling* (Fearn: Christian Focus Publications Ltd., 2002), 45.

[228]Ibid., 45; Welch, *Blame it on the Brain: Distinguishing Chemical Imbalances, Brain Disorders, and Disobedience*, 36.

[229]Pryde and Needham, *A Biblical Perspective of What to Do When You Are Abused By Your Husband*, 28.

whatever comes out of a person's heart that defiles him or her. It is what a woman in an emotionally abusive marriage is saying to herself in her heart that determines her response to the abuse.[230]

Usually, women in emotionally abusive marriages have peace in the home as one of the most important priorities in their lives, even if this means tolerating evil on the part of their husbands.[231] She may crave to be loved so much that she tolerates her husband's abusive behaviour, hoping that by doing so she will win his love.[232] Or, she may believe that she can no longer handle her situation and give up.[233] The wife builds patterns of thinking and behaviour based on what she tells herself when her husband is treating her in an abusive way.[234]

Instead of thinking and functioning in this way, the wife is to

---

[230]Ibid.

[231]Ibid., 29; Hendrickson, "Counseling Victims of Spousal Abuse," *Institute for Biblical Counseling & Discipleship,* mp3, http://www.ibcd.org/resources/messages/counseling-victims-of-spousal-abuse/ (accessed January 16 2014).

[232]Pryde and Needham, *A Biblical Perspective of What to Do When You Are Abused By Your Husband,* 29.

[233]Lou Priolo, "Biblical Resources for the Wife's Protection," *The Lou Priolo Audio Library,* CD LP40.

[234]Priolo, "How to Respond to Rejection and Hurt," *The Lou Priolo Library.*

live according to her purpose in life, which is to glorify Christ. This will involve her having the mind of Christ. This means that all of her desires, thoughts, and beliefs should be brought into alignment with the mind of Christ.[235] Up until now, she has been accepting what her husband says to her. Since she wants her thinking to glorify Christ, she will test any accusations, insinuations, exaggerations, twisting of facts, and/or use of guilt by what the Bible teaches about who Christ is, what he says about her, and what he says about how she should live. After testing what her husband has said with what the Bible says, she should believe and apply biblical teaching on these matters in her life.

There are a number of heart issues that she will be tempted to experience when she is treated in an emotionally abusive manner by her husband. Christ has answers for each of these issues in scripture.

Confusion and Doubt

Understanding that she is to have the mind of Christ will help

---

[235]Pryde and Needham, *A Biblical Perspective of What to Do When You Are Abused By Your Husband*, 28.

the wife come out of the state of confusion and doubt that she has been in. Instead of blindly believing whatever accusations her husband makes about how bad she is, she is to live in and through Christ. By doing so she will, for example, see when her husband tries to shift blame onto her.[236] If he denies having done or said something which he did say or do, she will not accept his denial at face value as being the truth.[237]

Living in order to glorify Christ will lead her away from being confused by changes in his behaviour. Switches from being loving and charming to angry and cruel, will lose their hold over her. Her motive will no longer be to try to ensure that he starts to behave in a kind way toward her, nor try to stop his cruel behaviour, since she will be focused on how to live and relate to him in a way that honours Christ. In time she will therefore no longer be susceptible to his mind-games, will stop second-guessing how her husband will respond to her, will no longer doubt her own ability to perceive reality as a human being, nor will she continue to blame herself

---

[236]Needham, "Abuse, Recognizing It," *Institute for Biblical Counseling and Discipleship.*

[237]Tim Jackson, "Emotionally Destructive Marriages," *RBC Webinars,* May 3rd 2014 http://helpformylife.org/2014/03/05/the-emotionally-destructive-marriage-webinar (accessed July 13, 2014).

for everything.[238] The result of this new way of living will be that her husband will no longer be able to control the thinking of his wife, nor blame her for everything because she thinks in a way that is pleasing to Christ.

Worry

Description

Worry involves being preoccupied with or "overly concerned" about something.[239] The main passages in scripture that address the issue of worry are Matthew 6:19-36 and Philippians 4:4-9.

Biblical Instruction for Dealing with Worry

Matthew 6:19-36 instructs believers to not lay up treasure on earth. They are instead to lay up treasure in heaven where it cannot

---

[238]Margaret Rinck, *Christian Men Who Hate Women* (Grand Rapids: Zondervan, 1990), 186.

[239]George Scipione, "Worry," *CCEF – West San Diego 92*. CD ibc9233.

be destroyed. We can discover what a person's treasure is by finding out what it is that he or she worries about. A woman in an emotionally abusive relationship will be tempted to worry about how to ensure that her husband is not angry with her, other people, or things in life that do not work out as he desires. She will probably worry about how to gain his love and acceptance, how she can survive (both mentally and financially) if he would leave her, and about the children suffering in some way if her husband would choose to punish then because he is angry at her (or them) for some reason.

This passage teaches us that the believer is not to worry because God cares for his creation. Since people are of much more value than the birds and flowers of creation that he cares for, she can be certain that God will take care of her. Instead of worrying about these issues, she is instead to seek God's kingdom first in her life.

Philippians 4:4-9 instructs believers to rejoice in the Lord, to not be anxious but prayerful, and to think in a way that honours God. To help the woman rejoice in the Lord, she could list God's attributes and think about how this aspect of who God is relates to whatever she is worrying about. In addition, she could write down what God has done in her life up until the present day.[240] Seeing the way in which he has cared for her and worked in her life in the past, will help her be certain that the Lord will keep his promises in relation to the issues that are a concern to her in the present and in the future.

Instead of giving in to the natural tendency to be preoccupied with these concerns, she can learn to pray about them to the Lord in a thankful way. Her thankfulness is toward the Lord because she knows that the Lord will care for her. When she does this, God promises that his peace will guard her mind and heart. Peter gives similar teaching. He instructs believers "humble yourselves, therefore, under the mighty hand of God so that at the proper time he may exalt you, casting all your anxieties on him, because he cares for you" (1 Peter 5:6, 7 ESV).[241]

To have the mind of Christ and to glorify him in her situation, the woman should think about what is true, honourable, just, pure, lovely, commendable, excellent, and praiseworthy

---

[240] Ibid.

[241] Ibid.; Elyse Fitzpatrick, "Christ's Word to Worriers," *Institute for Counseling and Discipleship.* Summer Institute 2011, mp3.

(Philippians 4:8). She could make a list of the thoughts that she has when she worries and ask herself if these thoughts correspond with the types of thoughts described in this verse. Instead of being preoccupied with these worrying thoughts, she should think about how God's attributes and promises are true regarding those specific issues that she is worrying about. In this way, she will think in a way that corresponds with this verse.

God's attributes are the characteristics of God that constitute his nature.[242] The following are a number of his attributes: he is omnipresent (Jeremiah 23:23-24; Psalm 139:7-10), omniscient (1 John 3:20; Psalm 139:1-2, 4, 16), wisdom (Romans 16:27; 1 Corinthians 1:24, 30; Ephesians 3:10), faithful (Deuteronomy 32:4), good (Luke 18:19; Psalm 100:5; Psalm 106:1; Psalm 107:1; Psalm 34:8); and love (1 John 4:8; John 3:16; Galatians 2:20). He is merciful (2 Corinthians 1:3), gracious (Romans 3:24; 2 Corinthians 8:9; Ephesians 2:8), holy (Psalm 71:22; 78:41; 89:18; Isaiah 1:4; 5:19, 24; 6:3; 1 Peter 1:16) and righteous (Deuteronomy 32:4). God is jealous (Exodus 34:14; Deuteronomy 4:24; 5:9), wrathful

---

[242]Erikson, *Christian Theology*, 265.

(Exodus 32:9-10; Deuteronomy 9:7-8; 29:23; 2 Kings 22:13; Romans 1:18), omnipotent (Psalm 24:8; Genesis 18:14; Jeremiah 32:27; Revelation 1:8), and longsuffering (Exodus 34:6; Psalm 86:15; Romans 2:4; 9:22; 1 Peter 3:20; 2 Peter 3:15).[243]

Fear

Description

A woman in an emotionally abusive marriage will be living in fear of what her husband might do to her and of speaking about him in a negative way to others. This means that she will probably be afraid of speaking to her church leaders about the way in which her husband treats her at home. Many women in such situations believe that they would be disloyal to their husbands if they were to tell others about how he treats her.[244]

The fear that she experiences may be the result of direct or

---

[243]Grudem, *Systematic Theology: An Introduction to Biblical Doctrine*, 173, 174, 190, 193, 195, 197-206, 216; Berkhof: *Systematic Theology*, 71-73.

[244]Pryde and Needham, *A Biblical Perspective of What to Do When You Are Abused By Your Husband*, 27; Hendrickson, "Counseling Victims of Spousal Abuse," *Institute for Biblical Counseling & Discipleship*.

veiled threats that he has made toward her, or what she imagines in her mind might happen to her if she upsets him too much.[245] Anyone who lives in fear becomes paralyzed from taking action.[246] Since she is dependent on her husband both mentally and probably financially, she will fear being rejected or abandoned by him because she will think that she will not be able to survive without him.[247]

Fear of Man

This type of fear is called the fear of man. Fear of man is "any anxiety that is caused by real or imagined discomfort, rejection, or danger being imposed on another human being."[248] It involves trying to ensure that one does not upset people more than being

---

[245]Pryde and Needham, *A Biblical Perspective of What to Do When You Are Abused By Your Husband*, 60; Needham, "Abuse. Recognizing It," *Institute for Biblical Counseling & Discipleship;* Needham, "Abuse. Addressing It; *Institute for Biblical Counseling & Discipleship.*

[246]Pryde and Needham, *A Biblical Perspective of What to Do When You Are Abused By Your Husband,* 60; Priolo, "Helping People Pleasers," *National Association of Nouthetic Counselors.*

[247]Rinck, *Christian Men Who Hate Women,* 87; Priolo, "Helping People Pleasers," *National Association of Nouthetic Counselors.*

[248]Pryde and Needham, *A Biblical Perspective of What to Do When You Are Abused By Your Husband,* 59.

concerned with honouring God. It is an "inordinate desire for people's approval" or an "inordinate fear of their rejection."[249] People who fear others will study their body language and likes and dislikes. They are unlikely to question the views of others and will react to conflict by giving in, withdrawing, or steering the conversation onto another topic.[250]

Fear of God

The person who fears man will struggle to fear God. Knowing who God is conquers the fear of man. Understanding his providence over believers is important.

God's providence is as follows:

> "God is continually involved with all created things in such a way that he (1) keeps them existing and maintaining the properties with which he created them; (2) cooperates with created things in every action, directing their distinctive properties to cause them to act as they do; and (3) directs them to fulfil his purposes."[251]

---

[249]Priolo, "Helping People Pleasers," *National Association of Nouthetic Counselors.*

[250]Ibid.

[251]Wayne Grudem, *Systematic Theology: An Introduction to Biblical Doctrine* (Leicester: Inter-varsity Press, 1994), 96-97.

Trusting that God directs all things to fulfil his purposes, helps the person who is inclined to fear to trust God that he is in control and working according to his plan in his or her life. Instead of living according to the belief that her husband is in control, the wife can trust the sovereign, providential God who is working toward his goal in her life.

A woman who fears God understands that she is by nature unclean and should be punished by the holy God. She also fears God because having trusted Christ, she has been made righteous by him. Understanding the work of Christ on the cross will lead her to worship and trust him.[252]

Trusting the God of Scripture

To fear God, the wife must know who God is by what he reveals of himself through scripture. In the Bible we discover that fear originated in Genesis 3:7-8, when Adam and Eve hid from each other and from God after they had disobeyed his command not to eat

---

[252]Welch, *When People Are Big and God is Small,* 96-97.

from the tree of the knowledge of good and evil.[253] Later, Israel gave in to fear in Numbers 13, when the people feared the giants of the land instead of trusting God and entering the Promised Land. In Deuteronomy, God tells Moses not to be afraid of Og, the king of Bashan, because the Lord had already given him into his hand (Deuteronomy 3:2). Moses instructs Joshua not to fear the other nations because the Lord would fight for him (Deuteronomy 3:22), and tells the people not to be afraid of the nations. Instead of being fearful, they were to remember what the Lord did to Pharaoh (Deuteronomy 7:17-18).[254] Joshua was commanded not to be afraid of the nations because the Lord was with him (Joshua 1:9). He then instructed the chiefs of the men not to be afraid but to be courageous, as the Lord would help them against their enemies (Joshua 10:25).[255]

David feared God rather than man. He wrote about fear in many of his Psalms. For example, in Psalm 23:4 he wrote that he feared no evil because the Lord was with him whose rod and staff comforted him. In Psalm 27:1-2, David refused to fear his enemies

---

[253] Ibid., 24.

[254] Ibid., 57-58.

[255] Ibid., 58.

because the Lord was his light, salvation, and stronghold.[256] In Psalm 3, although David knew that his enemies surrounded him, he trusted the Lord as his protector.

In Jeremiah 17:5-8, the person who trusts in other people is described as someone who will suffer and not prosper. In contrast, the person who trusts the Lord is blessed and leads a fruitful life.[257]

The wife should be helped to place her trust in God who is with her, cares for her, protects her, and is providentially bringing about his plan in her life. This will help her to focus on living for the glory of God instead of filling her mind with fearful thoughts of what her husband might or might not do, or what might or might not happen to her and her family, if she were to behave in some way that would upset him too much.

---

[256]Ibid., 60.

[257]Ibid., 70.

Guilt

Description

An emotionally abusive husband will blame his wife for her sin and failures, as well as for his own sin, failure, and guilt.[258] If she accepts the blame for these areas in his life, she will come to believe, as her husband already does, that if she had not said or done certain things, he would not have treated her in the way that he did.[259]

The Importance of Justification

The emotionally abused wife must understand the work of Christ on the cross. She will need to be aware that she is by nature a sinner who deserves to be punished (Romans 3:10, 23) and to see that through Christ's death on the cross she has been made righteous before God (2 Corinthians 5:21; Romans 3:24; 8:30). She should be helped to live out of this righteous standing before God. Since she is

---

[258] Pryde and Needham, *A Biblical Perspective of What to Do When You Are Abused By Your Husband*, 26.

[259] Hendrickson, "Counseling Victims of Spousal Abuse," *Institute for Biblical Counseling & Discipleship*.

in Christ, there is no condemnation for her (Romans 8:1). She has to learn to reject the condemnatory speech from her husband because God has justified her and Christ is seated at the right hand of God and is interceding for her (Romans 8:33, 34).

The Role of Sanctification

Being justified in Christ, the wife is called to become like him in her character. She is to put off her old self, renew her thinking, and put on the new self, created after the righteousness of God (Ephesians 4:22-24). If she is harbouring, for example, anger, malice, strife, or jealousy in her heart (Colossians 3:8; Galatians 5:20; 1 Peter 2:1), she should be helped to see that these belong to the old nature and to come to a place where she is able to repent of these heart attitudes.

Even though she is experiencing distress and suffering, she should feel guilty if she has these attitudes, or if she is sinning in behaviour toward her husband, such as speaking to him in a corrupting way (Ephesians 4:29). The fact that God is for her in Christ means that if she confesses her sins, she will be forgiven by him. He is her advocate with the Father who is faithful and just (1 John 1:9-2:3).

The wife should not accept condemnation from her husband since Christ died to take away her condemnation and is for her. By repenting of her personal sin, guilt is removed from her life. If she were to accept her husband's accusations or insinuations as being true, or the blame for his mistreatment of her however, there is no solution for the resultant guilt that she will feel. The reason for this is because she is not the cause of his behaviour and what he says about her is not true. The wife is not to blame for his behaviour, which means that she cannot be the solution for bringing about change in his thoughts, emotions, or behaviour.

We see the importance of the wife renewing her mind so that it reflects Christ and questioning what her husband says by testing it with scripture. The wife should only accept, in her thinking and behaviour, what is true in scripture.

Anger

Description

Women in emotionally abusive relationships often struggle with anger. Anger is a "whole-personed response of negative moral judgment against perceived evil."[260] Although the temptation to anger is a reaction to the way that her husband treats her, any sinful anger on her part comes forth from her own heart. It involves both mental judgment of perceived evil and an emotional response to that evil.[261]

The Anger of God

Not all anger is sinful. We read in the Bible that God was angry. For example, he was angry at Moses when he asked that someone else lead Israel out of Egypt (Exodus 4:14), the Psalmist warns against making the Son angry (Psalm 2:12), and Jesus was angry when he saw people making a profit at the temple instead of it

---

[260] Jim Newheiser, "Anger/Abuse," *Institute for Biblical Counseling & Discipleship*.

[261] Pryde and Needham, *A Biblical Perspective of What to Do When You Are Abused By Your Husband*, 45.

being a place of worship (John 2:13-17).[262] His anger was due to the sin of the people.

Human Righteous Anger

People can experience righteous anger. This is due to a sense of justice that people have because they are made in the image of the just God. When we see injustice, we want to see justice happen. In order for anger to be righteous however, it must involve the following: (1) a sin that has occurred; (2) a concern for the glory of God, not one's own glory; and (3) a righteous expression.[263]

Human Sinful Anger

Human anger is usually sinful, flowing forth from the corrupt heart.[264] James 4:1-3 teaches that anger comes from thwarted desires. The underlying attitude of the angry person is

---

[262]Newheiser, "Anger/Abuse," *Institute for Biblical Counseling & Discipleship.*

[263]Ibid.

[264]Pryde and Needham, *A Biblical Perspective of What to Do When You Are Abused By Your Husband,* 45.

that he or she wants something, needs something, or is convinced that he or she deserves something.[265] The angry person wants something so much that he or she is willing to sin in order to get it and to sin because he or she does not have it.[266] This means that anger is usually a sinful response to not getting what one desires or longs for (James 1:13-15).[267]

Helping the Emotionally Abused Woman Deal with Anger

To help a woman in an emotionally abusive marriage, we must help her see that her anger comes from her own heart. Understanding this and working on what is going on in her heart, will mean that she can live differently in her situation. She is called to conquer her anger (Proverbs 16:32; 25:28; James 1:19; Proverbs 22:24-25; Ephesians 4:31-32).[268] If her anger is sinful, we must help

---

[265]Ibid., 47.

[266]Priolo, "Counseling Angry People," *The Institute for Biblical Counseling & Discipleship.*

[267]Ibid.

[268]Pryde and Needham, *A Biblical Perspective of What to Do When You Are Abused By Your Husband,* 50.

her gain insight into what it is that she desires so much that she is sinning in her heart because that desire has not been met.

She can discover this by asking herself a few questions: what circumstances led to my becoming angry, what did I say and do when I became angry, what did I say to myself when I became angry, and what do I want from other people? She may desire to be respected, for him not to order her around, for him to show her love, for him to be less angry at her, for him to control his speech, for him to acknowledge wrongdoing in his past, or for him to have less mood swings.

She should confess those desires that have become too important for her and prayerfully seek to pursue God's desires instead. From here she should be helped to discover and apply what the Bible says about her and about what she should do in her situation. For example, Romans 12:14-21 teaches her to never repay evil for evil, to never seek revenge, and to refuse to be overcome by evil but to overcome evil with good. By doing this, she will be freed from seeking personal revenge because she knows that it is God who will punish sin.[269] When helping the emotionally abused woman to do this, it is important to remember that this is something that is extremely difficult to do and is only possible with the Lord's enabling. The helper's attitude toward the woman should be one of patience, compassion, and humility.

If she does suffer for doing good, instead of fearing her husband and being troubled, she can focus on regarding Christ as holy instead. Living in the strength of Christ will enable her to speak in a gentle and respectful way and keep her conscience clear as well (1 Peter 3:13-17). Instead of living for her passions, she will live for the will of God (1 Peter 4:1-2). She can do this because she knows that she is receiving the salvation of her soul and can glorify Christ in her response to suffering, while she waits upon her guaranteed heavenly inheritance (1 Peter 1:3-9).

---

[269] Justin Holcomb and Lindsay Holcomb, *Rid of My Disgrace: Hope and Healing for Victims of Sexual Assault* (Wheaton: Crossway, 2011), 132.

Shame

Description

A person experiences shame as a result of thinking that he or she is a failure. The shame-filled wife believes that she is unable to live up to her husband's standard due to something that is wrong with her as a person.[270]

Since the shame is due to some kind of perceived failure in her person, she will never be able to achieve the desired standard he has for her, and is, therefore, by nature inadequate.[271] As well as failing to achieve the standard that her husband has for her, her shame can also be because of her own behaviour, what was done to her by other people, or something related to her which is seen by the abuser as being inferior to him. For example, the abuser may believe that she is inferior to him simply because she is a woman.[272]

---

[270] Steven Tracy, *Mending the Soul: Understanding and Healing Abuse* (Grand Rapids: Zondervan, 2005), 74.

[271] Ibid., 75.

[272] Welch, *Shame Interrupted: How God Lifts the Pain of Worthlessness and Rejection*, 2.

Abusers use shame to have control over the victim.[273] In the process, they are able to shift their own guilt onto the victim by blaming the victim for their behaviour.[274]

Shame in the Bible

We first see shame in the Bible in Genesis 3:7, when Adam and Eve covered themselves because they were naked.[275] This is in contrast to Genesis 2:25, when Adam and Eve experienced no shame about being naked during the period of innocence before the fall in Genesis 3.[276] The human experience of shame is a result of the guilt of sinning against God.[277]

The shame of nakedness is seen in again in 2 Samuel 10:4, when Hanun shamed David's men by stripping them of their

---

[273]Ibid., 22; Tracy, *Mending the Soul: Understanding and Healing Abuse,* 76.

[274]Ibid., 85.

[275]Rinck, *Christian Men Who Hate Women,* 94; Welch, *Shame Interrupted: How God Lifts the Pain of Worthlessness and Rejection,* 46.

[276] The teaching in this section is largely based on Ed. Welch, *Shame Interrupted: How God Lifts the Pain of Worthlessness and Rejection* (Greensboro: New Growth Press, 2012).

[277]Leland Ryken, James Wilhoit, and Tremper Longman, ed. *Dictionary of Biblical Imagery: An encyclopedic exploration of the images, symbols, motifs, metaphors, figures of speech and literary patterns of the Bible,* 780.

clothes.[278] In this case, the shame experienced was a result of a deliberate attempt by Hanun's men to humiliate David's men.[279]

Christ Removes Shame

Christ is the answer for the shame victim of emotional abuse. In the gospels, we see that Jesus associated with those who were shamed by others because they were seen to be inferior. Examples are the woman at the well (John 4:1-45) and the tax collectors and sinners (Matthew 9:9-13).[280]

By dying on the cross, Jesus died in a shameful way, being naked and exposed to everybody who was looking at him.[281] He fulfilled Isaiah 53:3-5, knowing the shame of being "as one from whom men hide their faces, he was despised, and we esteemed him

---

[278]Ibid., 582.

[279]Ibid., 780.

[280]Welch, *Shame Interrupted: How God Lifts the Pain of Worthlessness and Rejection*, 137; Holcomb and Holcomb, *Rid of My Disgrace: Hope and Healing for the Victims of Sexual Assault*, 94.

[281]Welch, *When People are Big and God is Small: Overcoming Peer Pressure, Codependency, and the Fear of Man*, 66.

not."[282] Even though he was innocent, he suffered shame so that others would be made righteous. Through his death and resurrection on the cross, Jesus cancelled the debt that is against the abuse victim (Colossians 2:14). As a result of Jesus' death on the cross, when he became sin, the emotional abuse victim has become the righteousness of God (2 Corinthians 5:21). She has been justified by faith through Christ (Romans 5:1). There is now no condemnation for her (Romans 8:1) and is to live according to God's plan for her, by being holy and blameless before him (Ephesians 1:4).

Helping the Shamed Wife

The victim should be helped to see that she is righteous in Christ because of his work on the cross. Her shame has been borne by him, so that she will live a godly life. She should live out of the reality that her alienation from God has been removed by Christ so that she may be holy and blameless before him (Colossians 1:21,

---

[282]Holcomb and Holcomb, *Rid of My Disgrace: Hope and Healing for Victims of Sexual Assault,* 94.

22).

Instead of accepting her husband's judgment of her, she should be helped to see herself as Christ does. By nature she is a sinner who does not match God's perfect standard and is cut off from God. As a believer, she has been clothed with the righteousness of Christ because of his work on the cross. She belongs to Christ, even if her husband rejects and excludes her. The victim of emotional abuse can know that Christ has removed her shame in a personal, intimate way. In Isaiah 54:4-6, the LORD comforts Israel by saying that she is to forget her shame, as he, her Maker, is her husband. This is true of the church, the bride of Christ (Revelation 21:1-4). The victim of emotional abuse is part of the bride of Christ. She is to live out of the truth that, in him, she is holy and without blemish (Ephesians 5:27).

Loneliness

Description

Loneliness is an emotionally painful sense of not being connected to others. The lonely person may feel alone, unwanted, isolated, and left out.[283] In an emotionally abusive marriage, loneliness may be the result of living in fear, being isolated from others, a lack of intimacy with God, a lack of emotional connection with others, and a sense of being rejected by her husband.

Examples of Loneliness in the Bible

There are many examples of lonely people in the Bible. In 1 Kings 19:10, Elijah was in a state of great distress. He believed that he was left alone to serve the Lord. David's soul waited in silence for God alone. He knew that his hope was only in him (Psalm 62:5). There was no other person who took notice of him, or took care of his soul (Psalm 142:4). Asaph had no one on earth or heaven besides God (Psalm 73:25, 26). Demas, Crescens, and Titus left Paul. It was only the Lord who stood by him during his first trial (2 Timothy 4:10, 16, 17). Those closest to Jesus deserted him (Mark 14:50), Peter denied him (John 18:15-18; 25-27), and Judas betrayed him (Matthew 26:47-50). He was alone during his suffering in the

---

[283]Somerville, Mary. "Coping with Loneliness." *National Association of Nouthetic Counselors*, Annual Conference, 2005, mp3.

Garden of Gethsemane (Matthew 26:36-46), and was forsaken by the Father when he hung on the cross (Matthew 27:46).[284]

Helping the Lonely Wife

The lonely wife must be reconnected to others. In a healthy marriage, it would be normal to advise her to seek an emotional connection with her husband, however this would not be wise in an emotionally abusive relationship. This is because it would make her more emotionally dependent upon and controlled by her husband and would, therefore, compound the problem.

Since her aim in life is to glorify God, we should encourage her to choose to live for him, regardless of how her husband treats her. Her aim is to love the Lord with her whole being (Matthew 22:37).[285] She will have fellowship with God and others as she walks in the light (1 John 1:3, 7).[286]

---

[284]Ibid., Wayne Mack, "Loneliness & Self-Pity#1: How to Handle Loneliness," *The Dr. Wayne Mack Library.* CDWM4191.

[285]Caroline Newheiser, "Helping Women who are Married but Lonely," *The Institute for Biblical Counseling and Discipleship,* Summer Institute 2013. mp3.

[286]Wayne Mack, "Loneliness & Self-Pity#1: How to Handle Loneliness." *The Dr. Wayne Mack Library.* CDWM4191

God has promised believers throughout the ages that he will not leave them nor forsake them, but will always be with them (Psalm 139:7-12; Isaiah 41:10; Matthew 28:20; Hebrews 13:5).[287] She can know an intimacy with God by living and trusting that God is her husband. He compared his people in the Old Testament to a wife deserted and grieved in spirit, as a wife of youth when she is cast off (Isaiah 54:5, 6). We read in Hosea that despite this, God betrothed his people to him in righteousness, justice, steadfast love, mercy, and faithfulness (Hosea 2:19, 20).[288] Believers continue to be described as the bride of God in the New Testament (Ephesians 5:31, 32; Revelation 21:2).

To overcome loneliness, it will also be important that she establishes relationships with other people. This will probably displease her husband as coming out of her isolation will result in him having less control over her. This means that she should be

---

[287] Mary Somerville, "Coping with Loneliness," *National Association of Nouthetic Counselors*; Caroline Newheiser, "Helping Women who are Married but Lonely," *The Institute for Biblical Counseling and Discipleship.*

[288] Ibid.

wise in how she seeks relationships with other people.[289]

Depression

Description

The depressed woman in an emotionally abusive relationship will probably believe that nothing in life has sense or purpose.[290] She might find no reason for doing things, not even for getting out of bed in the morning.[291] She will lack hope, have a negative attitude, and see the worst in situations and people.[292]

This state is a result of how she has dealt with and interpreted her marriage. It therefore shows what has been going on in her heart.[293] Some spiritual issues are involved. Examples of such

---

[289] Wayne Mack, "Loneliness & Self-Pity#1: How to Handle Loneliness." *The Dr. Wayne Mack Library*.

[290] Edward Welch, "Counseling Those Who Are Depressed," *The Journal of Biblical Counseling* 18, no. 2 (Winter 2000), 6.

[291] Ibid., 7.

[292] David Powlison, "The River of Life Flows Through the Slough of Despond," *The Journal of Biblical Counseling* 18, no. 2 (Winter 2000), 2.

[293] Edward Welch, "Words of Hope for Those Who Struggle with Depression," *The Journal of Biblical Counseling* 18, no. 2 (Winter 2000), 43.

spiritual issues are her faith, her relationship with Christ, how she deals with sin in her life, and how she interprets her life.[294] She may be feeling guilty for personal wrongdoing or for failing to satisfy her husband. She may be living in fear of being punished, rejected, or abandoned by him, be living in shame, believe that she needs her husband, is angry at how he is treating her, and responding wrongly to his bad treatment.[295]

Dealing with the Heart Issues Involved in Depression

As the emotionally abused woman lives her life for the purpose of glorifying Christ, she will need to deal with the issues of her heart.[296] She should admit that her attempt to win the love of her husband and his trust has superseded the place of the Lord in her

---

[294] Edward Welch, "Understanding Depression," *The Journal of Biblical Counseling* 18, no. 2 (Winter 2000), 13.

[295] Welch, "Words of Hope for Those Who Struggle with Depression," *The Journal of Biblical Counseling,* 43; Welch, "Understanding Depression," *The Journal of Biblical Counseling,* 21.

[296] Welch, "Words of Hope for Those Who Struggle with Depression," *The Journal of Biblical Counseling,* 41; Edward Welch, "Helping Those Who Are Depressed," *The Journal of Biblical Counseling* 18, no. 2 (Winter 2000), 26.

life.[297] Her loss of hope will be because her husband does not give her the love, respect, acceptance, and kindness that she longs for, despite adapting herself and living according to his standards, views, and desires.[298]

Knowing Christ as the Purpose in Life

We should read scripture with her that focuses on Christ.[299] She has hope because, in Christ, she has received everything that she needs to live in a godly way in her situation (2 Peter 1:3, 4). She knows the Father of all compassion and the God of all comfort (2 Corinthians 1:3, 4). She can regain hope in life because she knows that the God of hope desires that she abound in it and that he can use her suffering for good (Romans 15:4; 5:1-5).

She should be encouraged to rejoice in the Lord and to adjust her thinking so that she is focusing on what is true (Philippians 4:4-

---

[297]Edward Welch, *Depression: Looking Up from the Stubborn Darkness* (Greensboro: New Growth Press, 2011), 159.

[298]Ibid.

[299]Welch, "Understanding Depression," *The Journal of Biblical Counseling,* 14.

8).[300] To help her with this process, she could write down things that she will think about when she is tempted to think sad thoughts.[301] Other believers could become involved to help her think according to who God is, what he has done for her, and what he has promised her.[302] She can be given help regarding her use of time, starting with doing one responsible thing every day, to being able to follow a schedule for the whole week.[303] This scheduling should include set times for getting up in the morning and going to bed at night, eating, and exercising.

Honouring Christ in the Home

Speech

In the account of creation in Genesis 1, we read that God spoke creation into being (Genesis 1:3, 6, 9, 11, 14, 20, 24, 26). It is

---

[300] Welch, "Helping Those Who Are Depressed," *The Journal of Biblical Counseling,* 28; Wayne Mack, "Biblical Help for Overcoming Despondency, Depression," *The Journal of Pastoral Practice* II, no. 2 (1978), 36.

[301] Ibid., 47.

[302] Welch, "Understanding Depression," *The Journal of Biblical Counseling,* 13.

[303] Wayne Mack, "Biblical Help for Overcoming Despondency, Depression," *The Journal of Pastoral Practice,* 47.

God who gave human beings the ability to speak. Adam used this ability when he gave the animals names in Genesis 2 and when he exclaimed "bone of my bones and flesh of my flesh" when he was introduced to Eve.[304]

Language was abused by Satan when he spoke to Eve and asked her if God really did say that she should not eat of any tree in the garden. He then went on to claim that Adam and Eve would be like God, knowing good and evil, if they ate from the tree of the knowledge of good and evil. As a result of Adam and Eve's decision to disobey God and eat from the tree, human speech is affected by sin. We immediately see the effect of sin on human speech in the same chapter in Genesis when Adam and Eve blamed each other and God for their own behaviour (Genesis 3: 12, 13).

Believers' speech should be for the glory of Christ and the good of the other person (Colossians 4:6; Ephesians 4:29).[305] The language that a person speaks comes out of the heart of that person

---

[304] Adams, Jay. *Language of Counseling* (Stanley: Timeless Texts, 1981), 13.

[305] Ibid., 40.

(Mark 7:20-23; Matthew 12:34).[306] This means that since the wife is working on the issues of her heart, and is seeking to live for the glory of God, she will be enabled by God to speak in an appropriate way to her husband, which humanly speaking seems like an impossible thing to do.[307]

If her husband verbally attacks her, she could say to him that she wants to communicate with him in a calm and productive way, not in an attacking manner. She should ask him to stop speaking to her in an attacking way. If he continues to do so, she should repeat what she has just said and add that she will leave the room if he does not stop. If he refuses to stop verbally attacking her, she should leave the room.[308] If he continues attacking her, she should leave the house. It is important that she creates physical distance between them. If, when discussing an issue with her husband, he starts to verbally attack her, accuse her, blame her, or divert the conversation onto something else, instead of being diverted, becoming defensive,

---

[306]Fitzpatrick, *Helper By Design: God's Perfect Plan for Women in Marriage*, 168.

[307]Newheiser, "Anger/Abuse," *Institute for Biblical Counseling & Discipleship*.

[308]Vernick, *The Emotionally Destructive Marriage*, 55; Jackson, "Emotionally Destructive Marriages," *RBC Webinars*.

or retaliating, she should stick to the issue being discussed by repeating what she was talking about in a polite and calm way.

All believers are called to care for one another and to confront fellow believers who are sinning (Galatians 6:1; Matthew 18:15), which means that it is right for her to confront her husband when he is sinning against her. Being passive and not confronting sin, will enable him to continue to treat her wrongly. As her husband's helper to become more Christ-like, she would not be fulfilling her role as his helper if she allowed him to relate to her in an angry, jealous, selfish, and controlling way. By confronting him about his sin, she is truly helping him because she is addressing issues in his life that do not correspond to the character of Christ.[309]

Boundaries

Preventing her husband from speaking to her in a harsh, angry, accusatory, or attacking manner, or from behaving in a way that punishes, harms, or attempts to intimidate is setting boundaries

---

[309]Hendrickson, "Counseling Victims of Spousal Abuse," *Institute for Biblical Counseling & Discipleship.*

around how she allows him to treat her. This is not selfish self-protection on her part, because she is setting limits so that he is not enabled to treat her in a way that is according to the old nature (Colossians 3:5-12; Galatians 5:19-21).[310] She is helping her husband by seeking to prevent him engage in behaviours that would hinder him from becoming Christ-like in his character. At the same time, she is ensuring that she is able to think and behave in ways that honour the Lord.

If he counters her ideas or feelings, she should not try to explain or attempt to get him to understand her. This is because he will just counter that explanation. All that she should do is repeat her original statement.[311] If he discounts what she says, she can say that she does not want them to communicate with each other in that way, but in a way that honours the Lord. Emotional abusers often make comments by joking. If he speaks in this way to her, she should not explain to him why she does not think that his joke was funny. Instead, she could ask him why he thinks it is right to make jokes

---

[310] Edward Welch, "Boundaries in Relationships," *The Journal of Biblical Counseling* 23, no. 3 (January 2004), 18.

[311] Evans, *The Verbally Abusive Relationship. How to Recognize it and How to Respond*, 136.

about such things.[312] When he denies that he has said certain things or treated her in a certain way, she should not try to explain to him what happened in an attempt to make him remember or understand. This is because he does understand and knows what happened. She should not believe him when he denies things, otherwise she will question her own ability to perceive reality.[313]

Doing Good

Living her life to the glory of God will mean that the emotionally abused wife will seek to glorify him in how she responds behaviourally toward her husband. Her motivating desire will be to not be overcome with evil, but to overcome evil with good (Romans 12:21).[314] Dealing with the issues of her own heart ensures that she herself is not overcome by evil. By doing good toward her husband, she is overcoming his evil with good.

---

[312]Ibid., 139.

[313]Ibid., 144.

[314]Priolo, "Biblical Resources for the Wife's Protection," *The Lou Priolo Audio Library;* Newheiser, "Anger/Abuse," Needham, "Abuse. Addressing It," *Institute for Biblical Counseling & Discipleship.*

Peter teaches likewise in 1 Peter 3:8-17. Instead of responding to evil with evil, and reviling with reviling, she should seek to bless her husband. This is only possible by the grace of God and the power of the Holy Spirit. This will mean that her speech will be good, she will pray, do good, and seek peace. In this way she will experience the Lord's blessing in her life. Good deeds include doing her daily tasks and seeking how to be a blessing to others. Other people includes her husband, any children they may have, and people outside the immediate family unit.

Importance of the Church

It is important for the wife to be involved in a church. As a Christian, she is part of the people of God, consisting of Jewish and Gentile believers (Ephesians 2:11-22). As a member of the people of God, she needs other people in the church to help her become a mature Christian. She especially needs teachers and shepherds to provide this kind of help (Ephesians 4:11-14).

As has been seen, emotional abusers often isolate their wives from other people. In this way, they are able to have control over them because there is no one who can say to her that what her husband is saying or doing is not normal. The church is important for the wife because she will hear teaching about the Lord, how she should think, and how she should live. This teaching should help her be able to grow in the Lord in her situation. For example, if she is taught by others that she is justified in Christ (Romans 5:1), is no longer condemned because she is in him (Romans 8:1), and that no condemnation or charge against her will stand (Romans 8:33, 34), she will be able to reject accusatory and condemning speech by her husband.

Having other people in her life who can teach her how to deal with any negative thoughts she may have, such as being a failure or a bad wife, will help her live as the Bible teaches rather than come under the control of her husband.[315] Being in relationship with other people, means that she will not be isolated. This lack of isolation has the potential to prevent his control to an extent.[316] This is especially true if there are people in the church who know about her situation,

---

[315] Tracy, *Mending the Soul: Understanding and Healing Abuse,* 90.

[316] Vernick, *The Emotionally Destructive Marriage,* 124.

who believe her, and do not take his good behaviour in public at face value. Where possible, she should seek to use her gifts to help others, thereby fulfilling her calling to use her gifts and to love others (Romans 12:3-13; Matthew 22:39).

Living Purposefully

The purpose in life for the wife in an emotionally abusive relationship is to live for the glory of Christ. Her identity is in him. She is to relate to her husband for the glory of Christ and out of her identity in him. In the Bible, a wife is called to be submissive to her husband, however her submission is to the Lord first. If her husband asks her to sin, or is asking something that would prevent her from living to the glory of Christ, or is enabling him to sin against her, she should not be submissive. In non-moral areas, she needs wisdom to know where being submissive to him will lead to. If it leads to him having control over her, she should not be submissive, because nobody should be allowed to have control over her. Her heart, or moral core, will be changing as she conforms to Christ. Instead of living in confusion and doubt, worry, fear, guilt, anger, shame, loneliness, and/or depression, she can live for the glory of Christ. In the home, she can respond to his abusive speech by talking in a calm and loving way, while confronting him about his sin. She should set boundaries to prevent him from being able to sin against her and so that she is able to follow the Lord. Since she is a member of the people of God, the church is important for her as it helps her mature in the Lord, counters any falsehoods her husband may be teaching her, brings her out of isolation, and provides an opportunity for her to be a blessing to others.

Chapter Four

In the previous chapter, we discovered what it means for the wife in an emotionally abusive relationship to live in Christ. By doing so, she fulfills her purpose of glorifying him and living in her identity as a child of God. It is from this identity and purpose that she is called to relate to her husband.

This chapter will go beyond the wife as an individual to the role of the people of God (the church) in her life. The chapter will suggest how the church can provide practical and spiritual support. First, insights from researchers about the importance of community in the life of the abused will be given. Second, scriptural teaching about the nature and the role of the church will be provided. Third, suggestions will be made about how the church can support the emotionally abused wife. Lastly, an approach to church discipline of the husband will be explained.

Researchers' Insights Regarding the Importance of Community for Abused Women

Researchers of abuse have discovered that its victims are helped by participating in a community that encourages their general well-being.[317] When an abused woman is part of a community, she is brought out of her isolated position. It is this isolated position that helps to enable the husband to have control over her.[318] The community that the abused woman is part of is in a position to be able to speak into her life when it hears that she is succumbing to his mind games or to his false ideas about who she is.[319] Examples of such ideas are thoughts she might have that she is an inferior person to him simply because she is a woman or that she needs him to think on her behalf because she is inherently unable to think and make decisions herself. The community that the abused woman is part of should be one in which all forms of abuse are unacceptable and it is

---

[317]Loring, *Emotional Abuse,* 71; Nicols, Brittney. "Violence against Women: The Extent of the Problem." In *"Intimate" Violence Against Women. When Spouses, Partners, or Lovers Attack.*
[318]Miller, *No Visible Wounds: Identifying Nonphysical Abuse of Women By Their Men,* 54.

[319]Nicarthy, *Getting Free: A Handbook for Women in Abusive Situations,* 89.

known by everybody that abusive behaviour will not be tolerated.[320]

Scriptural Teaching about the Church

From early on in the scriptures, we read that God called people to have a special relationship with him. This began with the calling of Abraham in Genesis 12:1-3. God promised to bless Abraham and to make him into a great nation and that his descendants would inherit the land of Canaan (Genesis 17:1-8). The people of Israel are God's people who descended from their forefather Abraham.

In the New Testament, God's people is expanded beyond the people of Israel to also include Gentiles, or people from other nations. Those that were not part of his people, have now become his people through faith in Christ (1 Peter 2:10). Both Jewish and non-Jewish believers are equal in him (Galatians 3:28). God's people, the church, consists of people from different nationalities who are in

---

[320]DiddyAntai. "Controlling behavior, power relations within intimate relationships and intimate partner
physical and sexual violence against women in Nigeria." *BMC Public Health* 11:511(2011). http://www.biomedcentral.com/1471-2458/11/511 (accessed November 10, 2014).

Christ.[321]

Various images are used of the church in the New Testament. Grudem lists several images. There is God's family (1 Timothy 5:1-2; 2 Corinthians 6:18; Matthew 12:49-50; and 1 John 3:14-18), the bride of Christ (Ephesians 5:32; 2 Corinthians 11:2), and the branches of a vine (John 15:5). It is an olive tree (Romans 11:17-24), a field of crops (1 Corinthians 3:6-9), a building (1 Corinthians 3:9), and a harvest (Matthew 13:1-30; John 4:35). Other images are God's house (Hebrews 3:3-6), the pillar and bulwark of the truth (1 Timothy 3:15), and the body of Christ (1 Corinthians 12:12-27; Ephesians 1:22-23; 4:15-16; Colossians 1:18, 2:19).[322] It is also the temple, or the Jerusalem from above (Galatians 4:26; Hebrews 12:22; Revelation 21:2).

The Church as the Body of Christ

The image of the church as the body of Christ shows us that all believers are united to one another in relationship. This united

---

[321] Louis Berkhof, *Systematic Theology*, 15th ed.(Edinburgh: The Banner of Truth Trust, 2000), 553.

[322] Wayne Grudem, *Systematic Theology: An Introduction to Biblical Doctrine*, 1858.

relationship of each member of the body is to Jesus Christ. He is the head of the body and as such nourishes, feeds, and rules it (Colossians 1:18).[323]

Each member of Christ's body has been given spiritual gifts which are to be used to edify and to strengthen other people for the common good (1 Corinthians 12:4-31). It is through the use of spiritual gifts by fellow believers that the woman in an emotionally abusive marriage can be helped to fulfil her calling in life. Some spiritual gifts are of special importance.

Wisdom (1 Corinthians 12:8) is important for knowing what advice to give to her about how to live in her particular situation. Teaching is needed in order to know the Lord and how to live in a way that he desires. Exhortation is to be used to help the woman persevere in living God's way. Mercy is important for when she experiences particular difficulty or has made mistakes in response to his abuse (Romans 12:8).

---

[323]Berkhof, *Systematic Theology*, 557; Millard Erickson, *Christian Theology*, 13th ed. (Grand Rapids: Baker Book House, 1985), 1036.

The Church as the Temple of God

The church is called the temple of God (1 Corinthians 3:16; Ephesians 2:21, 22; 1 Peter 2:5).[324] This means that the Lord indwells the church and that the church is therefore holy. As members of God's temple, believers are called to live holy lives (1 Corinthians 6:19-20).[325] The woman being part of the temple of God means that she will live in a different way than her husband does, since he is not living in a holy way as she is. She will be becoming holy, which means that she will not be the person that he wants her to be. The fact that she is not allowing her husband to control her, but is instead living in a way to please Christ in the first place, means that she will need the help and support of other people in the church to be able to continue living in this way.

The Church as the Pillar and Ground of Truth

As the pillar and ground of truth, the church is to guard the

---

[324]Berkhof, *Systematic Theology*, 559.

[325]Erickson, *Christian Theology*, 1039.

truth and defend it against its enemies (1 Timothy 3:15).[326] This involves the church preventing the teaching of false doctrine (1 Timothy 1:3, 4; Titus 1:9-11). In relation to marriage, the church should ensure that its teaching regarding the nature and the role of the husband and wife is in accord with what the Bible teaches. Teaching about justification should be held in high regard because attempts are often made to ensure that victims of emotional abuse feel guilty. Effort is made to try to get them to think that they are bad as people because they do not achieve some kind of human standard set by the abuser.

The Church as the People of God

As the people of God (2 Corinthians 6:16), the church belongs to him.[327] This means that as a believer, the wife belongs to God in the first place. Since she is a member of the people of God, she should live in a way that honours and glorifies the Lord, including the way in which she relates to her husband.

---

[326]Berkhof, *Systematic Theology*, 558.

[327]Erikson, *Christian Theology*, 1035.

The Church as a Priesthood

Believers are priests (1 Peter 2:9; Hebrews 13:15-16).[328] This means that believers should intercede for the wife before the Lord so that she will continue and persevere in living in a way toward her husband that honours the Lord. They should also intercede that the Holy Spirit work on the husband's heart so that he becomes aware of his wrongdoing and comes to a place of godly repentance (2 Corinthians 7:10).

Relating to One Another

Many passages in scripture speak about the role that believers have one to another. For example, believers are to instruct one another (Romans 15:14), teach and admonish one another in all wisdom (Colossians 3:16), and encourage and build one another up (1 Thessalonians 5:11; Ephesians 4:12, 29).[329] Believers are to encourage one another to love and good works (Hebrews

---

[328]Grudem, *Systematic Theology: An Introduction to Biblical Doctrine*, 859.

[329]Ibid., 959; Berkhof, *Systematic Theology*, 598.

10:24-25).[330] This means that the church should be involved in the life of the emotionally abused woman to encourage and instruct her to live in a way that glorifies the Lord in her situation.

The Church as the Family of God

Church members are intimately connected to each other as members of the family of God and are called to relate to each other as they encourage older men as fathers, younger men as brothers, older women like mothers, and younger women like sisters (1 Timothy 5:1, 2). God is the heavenly father of all believers (Ephesians 3:14, 15; 2 Corinthians 6:18).[331] As the family of God, there should be love and fellowship between members of the church and the emotionally abused woman.[332] There should be an intimacy of relationship and care toward her regarding her situation.

---

[330]Grudem, *Systematic Theology: An Introduction to Biblical Doctrine*, 959.

[331]Ibid., 858.

[332]Ibid., 859.

Caring for the Weak

Believers are called to care for the weak in society. In the Old Testament, God's people were called to care for the fatherless, the widow, and foreigners as the Lord cared for them (Deuteronomy 10:17-19). In biblical times, widows and orphans had no male figure to provide for them, which meant that they were in an especially vulnerable position. We see this when Jesus raised a widow's son from the dead (Luke 7:11-17). Since she had no husband or son to provide for her, the widow had no means of survival.[333] Believers in the New Testament are to care for orphans and widows (James 1:27) and to provide for those who need clothing and food (James 2:14-17; 1 John 3:16-18).[334]

Many emotionally abusive husbands do not provide their wives with enough finances for themselves and for their children. These women are in a similar position to that of the orphans and widows in biblical times because they lack someone who will provide for them. It is therefore important that the church helps the

---

[333]Erikson, *Christian Theology,* 1057-1058.

[334]Ibid., 1058.

woman and children so that she is able to survive and care for herself and her children without having to yield to her husband's control in order to do so.

How the Church Can Help the Emotionally Abused Woman

There are a number of ways that the church can help the emotionally abused woman. When teaching about how people should relate to each other, the church can teach that trying to manipulate and control any human being is sinful and should have no place in the life of a believer or of the church. It should be made clear that any person who relates in this way to others, will be spoken to about it and helped to live differently.

Couples should be taught during pre-marital counselling about the nature of both the male and female as human beings before and after the fall. They should be taught what renewal in Christ means for them both individually and for their marriage. Church members should be taught how to change and live in a way that glorifies Christ.

The church should be a community that brings an

emotionally abused woman out of her isolated position. This will mean being involved in her life. The church can provide support by helping her take care of her children, doing practical jobs, and giving financial assistance and advice when needed. Believers can help her maintain clear thinking by showing her when she is thinking or believing things which do not accord with scripture and help her to renew it appropriately. By providing support and helping her renew her mind, church members are blocking the husband's attempts to control his wife. As a priesthood, believers should be interceding for her before the throne of God so that she perseveres in honouring the Lord in how she lives.

It might be necessary for the church to provide medical care and even legal advice. If the husband is making legal threats or using the law to manipulate his wife, the church should seek legal advice so that they know what the law actually says and how they can help the wife appropriately.

Church Discipline

One of the tasks of the church is that of practicing church

discipline. Church discipline involves different stages of confronting and dealing with erring, or sinning, church members. The church helps the woman in an emotionally abusive marriage by confronting the husband about the way that he is treating his wife.

The Purpose of Church Discipline

There are a number of purposes for church discipline. First, it is a refusal on the part of the church to tolerate sin in the lives of its members.[335] The church is the temple of God, and as such, is holy (1 Corinthians 6:19-20). As the dwelling place of God, the church is to be holy.[336] Believers are called to be holy because God is holy (1 Peter 1:16). Since members of the church take this calling seriously, they will confront believers who are not leading holy lives.

Second, by confronting sin in the lives of erring members, the church protects other members from engaging in an unholy lifestyle. Paul teaches in 1 Corinthians 5:6, 7 that the church is not to

---

[335] Jim Newheiser, "Church Discipline: 1 Corinthians 5," *Institute for Biblical Counseling & Discipleship*, mp3.

[336] Berkhof, *Systematic Theology*, 599.

tolerate sin because "a little leaven leavens the whole lump." Instead of tolerating sin, the church is to cleanse out sin in its midst so that it is pure.[337] Failure to discipline, as was the case with the church in Corinth regarding the man who was having sexual relations with his father's wife, is described in scripture as arrogance (1 Corinthians 5:2) and boasting (1 Corinthians 5:6).[338]

Third, by confronting sin in the lives of erring members, the church protects herself from coming under the judgment of God.[339] We read in Revelation 2:5 that the church at Ephesus was commanded to repent of abandoning its first love, otherwise its lampstand would be removed. In Revelation 2:16, the church in Pergamum was called to repent of allowing people to hold to the teaching of Balaam and of the Nicolaitans. If they would not repent, Jesus would come and war against them with the sword of his mouth. The church in Thyatira was warned in Revelation 2:22

---

[337]Newheiser, "Church Discipline: 1 Corinthians 5."; Jay Adams, *Handbook of Church Discipline: A Right and Privilege of Every Church Member* (Grand Rapids: Zondervan, 1974), 1; Grudem, *Systematic Theology: An Introduction to Biblical Doctrine*, 895.

[338]Adams, *Handbook of Church Discipline: A Right and Privilege of Every Church Member*, 895.

[339]Newheiser, "Church Discipline: 1 Corinthians 5."

that if Jezebel and her followers did not repent, they would be thrown on a sick bed. The church in Sardis was to repent of her incomplete works in Revelation 3:3, otherwise Jesus would come like a thief. Lastly, the church in Laodicea was called to buy gold refined by fire and white garments from Jesus since he reproves and disciplines those he loves (Revelation 3:19).

Fourth, church discipline is designed to bring about the restoration of the erring believer.[340] This is seen by the context surrounding the main teaching passage about this subject in Matthew 18:15-20. In the preceding verses, Jesus speaks about the importance of searching for the lost. He teaches that it is not the will of the Father that any of the little ones should perish (Matthew 18:10-14). These verses show that the restoration of the lost is on the heart of God.[341]

In Matthew 18:15-20, the process of church discipline is explained. When a brother is sinned against in private, he is to go to the offender and tell him about his fault. This first stage of church

---

[340] Ken Sande, "Redemptive Church Discipline," *Institute for Biblical Counseling & Discipleship,* Summer Institute, 2009, mp3; Grudem, *Systematic Theology: An Introduction to Biblical Doctrine,* 894.

[341] Ken Sande, "Redemptive Church Discipline."

discipline is done privately between the offended party and the offender. If the offender listens, he has been won. This shows that the purpose of going to the offender is to win and restore that person. Paul teaches in Galatians 6:1, 2 that if there is a situation where a person is caught in a transgression, spiritual people should restore that person in a spirit of gentleness. Jesus taught that when someone confronts another person about something that is wrong in his or her life, the confronter should have first examined and removed any sin themselves so that there is no hypocrisy involved and that the issues that are relevant to the person and the situation can be clearly seen (Matthew 7:1-5).[342]

If the offender does not listen when confronted, the offended party should take along one or two others so that "every charge may be established by the evidence of one or two witnesses" (Matthew 18:16). If the offending party refuses to listen to this group, the church is to be told (Matthew 18:17). If the offending party refuses to listen after the church has been told, the church is to treat him or

---

[342]Newheiser, "Church Discipline: 1 Corinthians 5.";Grudem, *Systematic Theology: An Introduction to Biblical Doctrine*, 894-899.

her as a Gentile and as a tax collector (Matthew 18:17). The determining factor for when church discipline is to move forward to the next stage is when the offending party demonstrates that he or she refuses to listen to what the others are saying.

For a person to be treated as a Gentile and a tax collector means that the person is to be considered as not belonging to Christ. In other words, he or she is to be treated as an unbeliever. He or she should no longer be allowed to partake of communion as that involves participating in being part of the church as a body (1 Corinthians 10:17). If there is any contact with the person by members of the church, they are to try to evangelize him or her by speaking about the gospel, forgiveness, and the grace of God.[343] Paul teaches us about how we are to treat people in such situations. He instructed the believers in Corinth that they were not to associate with anyone who calls himself a brother and is "guilty of sexual immorality or greed or is an idolater, reviler, drunkard, or swindler" (1 Corinthians 5:11). They were not even to eat with such a person. This means that the church is not to treat the offending party as they

---

[343] Sande, "Redemptive Church Discipline."

normally would as if nothing is wrong, but must change and limit contact with him or her.[344]

Jesus teaches in Matthew 18:18-20, that "whatever you bind on earth will be bound in heaven," and "whatever is loosed on earth will be loosed in heaven." He instructed the disciples that if "two or three of them agree about anything they ask, it will be done for them by the heavenly Father." The reason for this is because Jesus is among the two or three who are gathered in his name. This means that God is with believers as they are engaged in the process of church discipline. He gave the disciples his authority to "forgive and retain sins declaratively."[345] The church has been given the authority of Christ in this area.[346]

The process explained in Matthew 18:15-20 is for sins which are private. In other places in scripture, public sins are dealt with publicly. The first two stages of discipline are not needed. In 1 Corinthians 5:1-8, the sin of the man who was guilty of sexual

---

[344] Adams, *Handbook of Church Discipline: A Right and Privilege of Every Church Member*, 351.

[345] Berkhof, *Systematic Theology*, 599.

[346] Adams, *Handbook of Church Discipline: A Right and Privilege of Every Church Member*, 11.

immorality with his father's wife was public knowledge. Paul instructed the Corinthians that he should be removed from among them. He was to be "delivered to Satan for the destruction of the flesh, so that his spirit may be saved on the day of the Lord." A second example is in Galatians 2:11-14. Cephas was acting hypocritically and leading others to do the same by not eating with believing Gentiles when believing Jews were present. This was despite his regular practice of eating with Gentile believers at other times. In this situation, Paul rebuked Cephas in front of all the others about his hypocrisy and did not go to him first on his own as is the case with private sins according to Matthew 18:15-20.

The purpose of ex-communication from the church remains that of the restoration of the offending party. In 2 Corinthians 2:6-8, the Corinthians were instructed to forgive and comfort the sorrowful offender. They were to reaffirm their love for him.

When the offending party is repentant and is reinstated into the church community, he or she will need help regarding the issues that were involved. The person will also need help with re-establishing social contacts, reconciling with people he or she has sinned against in the past, discovering how to serve in the church, and possibly medical and financial issues.[347] It would be wise for the church to put accountability measures in place by providing counsel for the offending party in the areas that have been a source of difficulty.[348]

Church Discipline for the Emotionally Abusive Husband

When the church decides to confront the emotionally abusive husband about how he thinks about and treats his wife, it would not be wise for them to tell the wife that she must speak to him on her own about his behaviour and wait to see if he listens. This is because she will most probably have appealed to him about his way of treating her many times already. Since he has control over her mind, he might persuade her that she is the one who is in the wrong with the result that she takes no further steps to help her husband. He might also threaten her not to go back to the elders or might punish her for already having done so. The church leaders could ask her to

---

[347] Ibid., 10.

[348] Sande, "Redemptive Church Discipline."

keep a record of how he speaks to her and how he treats her. This is to ensure that other people believe her, see the seriousness of the situation, and can confront the husband with facts.

Many emotionally abusive men are popular, charming, and well-regarded outside of the home.[349] It is therefore likely that some people will not believe her that he can be such a different person toward her in the home. The motive for the wife keeping a record of his behaviour is not that of being vengeful or of dishonouring her husband. Her motive is wanting to help her husband come to repentance so that he is fulfilling his calling of reflecting the image of Christ.

When the husband is confronted by two or three others about his behaviour, measures should be taken to ensure that he does not punish his wife. They should inform him that they want her to talk to them about him and their relationship. They should also inform him that they will know that if she says at some future point that she

---

[349]Nicols, "Violence against Women: The Extent of the Problem." In *"Intimate" Violence Against Women. When Spouses, Partners, or Lovers Attack;* 3; Bancroft, *Why Does He Do That? Inside the Minds of Angry and Controlling Men,* 8.

should not have spoken to them, that it was a misunderstanding, that she was the one in the wrong, or that his behaviour toward her has changed, that he has been intimidating her and they will take the church discipline further.

When the husband is confronted, he should be reminded about what the Bible teaches about human nature in the image of God, sin issues in his life, and his responsibility to love his wife in a way that corresponds with what the Lord commands of him. He should be told that both he and his wife are created in the image of God (Genesis 1:26-28) and are therefore of equal value and worth. He should be taught that since Eve came from Adam's rib, she is of the same substance as him and is in no way inferior to him as a person. She is his helper to provide that which he lacks in himself. She helps him to be God's image bearer (Genesis 2:18-23).

The husband should be shown from Genesis 3:16, that ruling his wife is a result of sin. It is not a command from the Lord about how a husband ought to treat his wife. Since ruling his wife is sinful, he should repent of that way of relating to her. He should be shown that his belief that his wife meet his needs, has no needs of her own, and is married to him to gratify him, is selfish, wrong, and must be repented of.[350] He should be shown that instead of living with an entitled attitude, he is to love and cherish his wife as Christ did the church (Ephesians 5:25-29). He is not to be harsh with her (Colossians 3:19) and is to live with her "in an understanding way, showing honour to the woman as the weaker vessel" (1 Peter 3:7). It is important that he understand that the wife being weaker than the husband does not imply that she is inferior to him, since she is an heir together with him. The church leaders will need to show him that living in a jealous and angry way toward his wife is wrong, sinful and should be repented of (Galatians 5:20).

The church leaders should teach him that his wife is called to glorify Christ with her mind. She is to be renewed in the spirit of her mind (Ephesians 4:23) and to be transformed by its renewal so that she can discern the will of God (Romans 12:2). In the light of this teaching, he should be informed that it is wrong of him to want to control her mind. The mind of the wife should glorify Christ and not be controlled by her husband.

---

[350]Ibid., 111.

The husband should be confronted about the way that he speaks to his wife. Instead of engaging in verbal abuse, coercion and threats, minimizing, denying, and blaming, intimidation, and mind games, he should be shown his responsibility to speak in a way that reflects God's character and edifies his wife (Colossians 4:6; Ephesians 4:29). He should be confronted about how he behaves toward her regarding playing mind games with her, isolating her from other people, trying to have financial control over her, using the children to manipulate her, behaving differently outside the home than inside it, and behaving better in order to lead her to falsely believe that he has changed.

Someone, or some people, from the church could start to meet with the husband on a regular basis, such as every week, so that he is held accountable and to teach him how to change and live in a way that glorifies Christ toward his wife, in his home, and in all areas of his life.

Throughout the process, help should be given to the wife so that she too is living for the glory of Christ. If the husband is excommunicated and seen as a Gentile and a tax collector, the church will have to increase the support it provides for the wife.

The Supportive Church

This chapter suggested how the church can provide practical and spiritual support for the emotionally abused woman. Researchers of abuse have discovered abuse victims are helped by participating in a community that encourages their general well-being. By being part of a community, she is brought out of the isolated position she has been in that has enabled her husband to control her. The community is in a position to be able to speak into her life when it hears that she is succumbing to his mind games or to false ideas about who she is. The community should be one in which all forms of abuse are known to be unacceptable.

The church is God's people who have been called by him to be a community of believers. It is his body, a temple, the pillar and ground of truth, his people, his family and a priesthood. Church members are to serve one another and care for the weak.

Care and support can be given regarding emotional abuse by teaching about how people should relate to each other in a biblical way. Couples should be taught about human nature, marriage, and how to relate to other people during pre-marital counselling. All church members should be taught how to change and live in ways that glorify Christ. The church can bring an emotionally abused woman out of her isolated position by being involved in her life, providing practical support, and giving financial assistance and advice when needed. Older believers should help the woman with renewing her mind. Fellow believers should be interceding for her before the throne of God. It is possible that the emotionally abused woman may need medical care and legal advice.

The church can help the woman in an emotionally abusive marriage by using church discipline to confront the husband about the way in which he is treating his wife. Church discipline is a refusal on the part of the church to tolerate sin in the lives of its members. It protects other members from engaging in an unholy lifestyle and it protects the church from coming under the judgment of God. It is done in order to bring about the restoration of the erring believer. During the process of church discipline of the husband, the wife has to be provided with protection. The husband should be confronted about the way in which he thinks about and treats his wife. The church should teach him how to change and hold him accountable for doing so.

Chapter Five

Making it Practical

In this last chapter, we will turn again to the main principles given throughout the book. After restating the principles, suggestions will be made about how they can be applied when helping a woman in an emotionally abusive marriage. The chapter finishes with areas that have not been covered in this book and where there is need for biblical teaching.

The Nature of Emotional Abuse

Emotional abuse was defined as any non-physical behaviour that is designed to control, intimidate, subjugate, punish, or isolate another person resulting in the victim becoming emotionally, behaviourally, and mentally dependent on the abuser.

This means that there are men who use non-physical behaviours to control their wives and there are women who are emotionally, behaviourally, and mentally dependent on their husbands. It is important for the church, therefore, to be aware that there is a high likelihood that there will be marriages in the church where the husband controls his wife by using emotional abuse. If a husband and wife become Christians after marriage, it will be important for the church to be aware that there is a possibility that they relate to each other in this way.

The Types of Behaviours that are Involved with Emotional Abuse

A number of common behaviours that emotional abusers use include verbal abuse, coercion and threats, minimizing, denying, and blaming, intimidation, mind games, isolation, male privilege, financial control, using the children, exhibiting two personalities, jealousy, and good periods. The cumulative effect of these behaviours is that the husband gains control over his wife.

This implies that some men will speak to their wives in a verbally abusive way. They will use coercion, threats, minimizing, denying, blaming, intimidation and mind games. Teaching is needed in the church about speaking to other people, who are image-bearers of God, in ways that build them up and are for their good. It should be taught that the motive when speaking to another is not in order to get one's own way, rather it is to be for the good of the other. Believers should be taught that their speech should glorify God. This means that denying that something has happened, when that thing has happened, is deceitful and is not telling the truth. Believers are to be truth-tellers because they reflect the God who is truth.

Teaching should also be given that all believers are called to renew their thinking so that it glorifies Christ. It should be known in the church that it is wrong to use mind games. This kind of behaviour should be repented of. Husbands should be taught to encourage their wives to learn to think in ways that glorify Christ, even when that will mean that the wife does not think in exactly the same way as the husband does because she disagrees with him about something.

It is possible that there may be women in the church membership who are leading isolated lives because of being treated in an emotionally abusive manner by their husbands. The church can lovingly seek to discern if they are being treated in this way. If there is a woman in the church who is being emotionally abused, the church should ensure that she does have social and spiritual contact with other people. This contact should be such that other members of the church are aware of any attempt by the husband to isolate his wife or to confuse her thinking. The church members will then be in a position to help the wife think in a way that is biblical and corresponds with reality. In this way the husband's control over his wife will be blocked.

Sadly, there may be men in the church who abuse their position as heads over their wives in order to control them. Teaching should be given in the church that the Bible does not instruct husbands to rule over their wives, rather they are to love and cherish them. Their position as leader in the home is one of responsibility to love and care for others, not to rule and have one's own way. This kind of teaching should be given from the pulpit, during marriage counsel, and during pre-marital counselling.

Since there may be marriages in the church where the husband controls the finances and may not give his wife enough funds if she does not do what he says, teaching should be given from the pulpit, during marriage counsel, and during premarital counsel, that the husband is to financially provide for the wife. The church may need to help these women financially so that she is able to withstand his attempts to control her. It is possible that the wife may need to find paid employment so that she can care for her family.

It is also possible that there may be children in the church who are suffering because their fathers are punishing them in order to control their mothers. To help these children, those in the church who work with children should seek to relate them in a way that is loving and glorifies Christ. By doing so, they can gain the trust of the children and will hopefully become aware of what is going on in the home so that the family can be helped. Children's workers should be especially aware of children who are fearful and inhibited. Second, the church can provide childcare if the husband uses the children to prevent the mother from having paid employment. Third, the church can provide practical help for the mother by offering household help, help with the children's homework, and life's essentials such as food and drink.

There may be men in the church who appear to be spiritual men and upstanding citizens in the community, but have two personalities. If a woman confides about her husband's emotionally abusive behaviour, she should be taken seriously, regardless of how her husband behaves or is perceived in public.

When trying to help a woman who is being emotionally abused, it is to be expected that her husband will have good periods. These periods could lead her to gain hope that he has changed. It is important for counsellors to be aware that good periods belong to the behaviour pattern of an emotional abuser. This means that they will be cautious when advising her to believe that he has changed. While praying and hoping that this will genuinely take place, the church should wait for an extended period of time in order to see that the change has become a new pattern of behaviour.

The Effects of Emotional Abuse on the Victim

The effects of emotional abuse on the victims are confusion, doubt, fear, guilt, worry, inhibition, anger, shame, a changed mental state, emotional, behavioural, and mental dependence upon the abuser, physical ailments, loneliness, depression, and sorrow.

Many of the effects of emotional abuse are heart issues that all people struggle with at some point in their lives. Examples of such heart issues are doubt, fear, worry, anger, and shame. Counsellors should be aware that a woman suffering from such things might have more going on in her life than the majority of people do who suffer from them. When people in the church are helping women with these issues, they should gather information about the woman's whole life, and her responses to what she experiences. The information that is gathered might indicate that she is in an emotionally abusive relationship. The same is true for women who suffer from the emotional and physical effects of emotional abuse. If there is a woman in the church who exhibits the emotional issues above and has lasting physical health problems, such as chronic pain, those in the church who are involved with helping her should be aware that it is possible that she is in an emotionally abusive marriage.

A Biblical Approach for Helping Emotionally Abused Women

In chapter two we saw that men and women are made equally to reflect God and his rule over his creation. The woman was made from the man, being of the same substance as him, to be his helper and glory. As his helper, she provides him with strength that he does not have within himself. After Adam and Eve sinned, there has been a power struggle between them. Due to the work of Christ on the cross, the image of God in men and women that was marred by Adam and Eve's sin has been renewed. Male and female believers are dead to sin, alive to righteousness, and are called to reflect Christ in their characters.

Each is responsible before God for his or her own life, with Christ being the ultimate authority. In marriage, a wife is to choose to be submissive to her husband, however she is not to be submissive to sin, be complicit in it, nor tolerate her husband treating her in a sinful way. The husband, as head of the wife, is to love her as Christ loved the church, seeing her as his own body and respecting her as the weaker vessel. He is to serve and love her, not domineer and rule her.

This biblical understanding of the nature of men and women and how they are to relate to each other in marriage needs to be taught and seen in the church. Teaching should be given that people should be treated as equals, regardless of what that person's gender is or what he or she does in the church. Relationships in the church should exhibit equality of personhood. Older couples in the church should relate and demonstrate biblical ways of relating to others so that younger couples and new believers are shown by example how to have a biblical marriage.

Living in Christ and Fulfilling Life's Purpose

The purpose in life for an emotionally abused wife is to live for the glory of Christ and to live in her identity as a child of God. She is called to relate to her husband for the glory of Christ. In such marriages, the issue of submission is often abused by husbands as this helps them gain control over their wives. The wife's submission is to the Lord first. If her husband asks her to sin, asks her to do something that would prevent her from living for the glory of Christ, or if by being submissive she is enabling him to sin against her or to live in what is of the old nature, she should not be submissive. If the issue involved is not a moral issue, she should ask what being submissive would lead to. If it leads to him having control over her, she should not be submissive, as no human being should have a position of control over another. Living to the glory of Christ will mean that the core of her person, her heart, will be changed so that it conforms to him. In the Bible there are answers for how the Lord can change a heart that is inclined to confusion, doubt, worry, fear, guilt, anger, shame, loneliness, and/or depression. In the home, she can speak to her husband in a way that is honouring to the Lord and should confront him about the way that he relates to her. It is important that she set up boundaries to prevent him from being able to sin against her and so that she is able to follow the Lord. As a member of the church, she should be part of the community of believers so that she can mature in the Lord, renew her thinking, come out of her isolated position, and be a blessing to others.

Women in the church have to be taught and encouraged that their purpose in life is to live for the glory of Christ. When marriage counselling is given, the counsel should focus first on how the husband and wife as individuals relate to the Lord. Solving marital difficulties should be dealt with after discipleship is given regarding how to live for him.

There will be husbands in the church who domineer and manipulate their wives into being submissive to them. This means that counsellors have to be very careful when telling a wife to be submissive. The counsellor should begin with teaching her to live for the glory of Christ, not with whether or not she is being submissive to her husband. If a woman in an emotionally abusive marriage is advised to be submissive to her husband, the problem of emotional abuse will only be compounded as it is further enabling the husband to have control over her. If she is told that God wants her to be submissive, and that she has to be if she wants to obey the Lord, the counsellor has used the authority of God to compound the problem. This will affect her view of who God is because she will think that he wants her to accept such treatment.

As heart issues are worked on, the woman in the emotionally abusive marriage can change and live according to her purpose in life. The church should teach all believers how to change. If believers are taught this so that they are thinking, desiring, and behaving to the glory of the Lord, it prevents women from getting into the position of being emotionally abused.

In addition, women in emotionally abusive marriages should be encouraged to be actively involved in church. The woman should decide what activities to be involved in both for her own growth and in order to be a blessing to others. At no point should the woman be counselled to stay at home and no longer come to church. This would lead to isolation and the husband being able to have more influence over her mind since there are no other people to speak into her life regarding any strange ideas that she believes about herself or her life.

How the Church can Provide Support

The community of believers is important to bring the emotionally abused wife out of her position of isolation. The church is the body of Christ, his temple, the pillar and ground of truth, the people of God, the family of God, and a priesthood. Church members are to serve one another and care for the weak. Church discipline should be used toward the husband to bring him to repentance, to protect the church from the judgment of God, to protect other members from leading unholy lifestyles, and because the church should not tolerate sin. He should be confronted regarding the way he thinks about and treats his wife. It is important that the church hold him accountable during this process and that practical support and care is given to the wife.

The church is a community of believers who lead holy lives and help each other in spiritual and practical ways to do the same. It is to be a community where it is known that abuse, manipulation, and control will not be tolerated. It will be known that anybody who behaves in this way will be helped to change while undergoing the process of church discipline. The application is that the community of believers will be actively involved in each other's lives, knowing how their relationships, lifestyles, and relationship with God are. Relationships among believers should be encouraged to make this possible.

The church should be aware of the legal issues involved in abuse situations. For example, they should know what the legal rights of the children are, what financial responsibilities each partner has, what the legal ramifications are if one spouse leaves the home, and what they can and cannot do as a church. By being informed about the law in these areas, the husband will not be able to lie to either the church or his wife about what his position and rights are, or try to threaten people with legal action for becoming involved in his family life.

Pursuing Wisdom

This book has focused on how to how to help women in emotionally abusive marriages. There are a few areas that have not been covered. The first area is that of forgiveness. A vast amount of literature has been produced about the subject of forgiveness. Considerable thought needs to be done regarding the dynamics and application of forgiveness toward someone who asks for it but does so during a good period of abusive behaviour. Insight is required about how to advise the woman in this area.

The second area is that of the sexual relationship. In abusive marriages, sex is often used as a means of gaining power over the wife by the husband. How should counsellors advise a wife about the application of 1 Corinthians 7:3-5 when her husband uses sex as a means of having power over her?

The third area is that of physical abuse. Emotional abuse often develops into physical abuse. Help is needed for women who are being both emotionally and physically abused.

In closing, it is important to remember the depth of suffering experienced by these women. The emotional pain they go through because of being treated cruelly by their companion is close to being beyond words. David wrote about the hardship of being treated badly by a companion in Psalm 55. May these women cast their burdens on the Lord and experience him sustaining them.

Cast Your Burden on the Lord
To the choirmaster: with stringed instruments. A Maskil of David.

Give ear to my prayer, O God,
and hide not yourself from my plea for mercy!
2 Attend to me, and answer me;
I am restless in my complaint and I moan,
3 because of the noise of the enemy,
because of the oppression of the wicked.
For they drop trouble upon me,
and in anger they bear a grudge against me.
4 My heart is in anguish within me;
the terrors of death have fallen upon me.
5 Fear and trembling come upon me,
and horror overwhelms me.
6 And I say, "Oh, that I had wings like a dove!
I would fly away and be at rest;
7 yes, I would wander far away;
I would lodge in the wilderness; Selah
8 I would hurry to find a shelter
from the raging wind and tempest."
9 Destroy, O Lord, divide their tongues;
for I see violence and strife in the city.
10 Day and night they go around it

on its walls,
and iniquity and trouble are within it;
¹¹ ruin is in its midst;
oppression and fraud
do not depart from its marketplace.
¹² For it is not an enemy who taunts me—
then I could bear it;
it is not an adversary who deals insolently with me—
then I could hide from him.
¹³ But it is you, a man, my equal,
my companion, my familiar friend.
¹⁴ We used to take sweet counsel together;
within God's house we walked in the throng.
¹⁵ Let death steal over them;
let them go down to Sheol alive;
for evil is in their dwelling place and in their heart.
¹⁶ But I call to God,
and the LORD will save me.
¹⁷ Evening and morning and at noon
I utter my complaint and moan,
and he hears my voice.
¹⁸ He redeems my soul in safety
from the battle that I wage,
for many are arrayed against me.
¹⁹ God will give ear and humble them,
he who is enthroned from of old, Selah
because they do not change
and do not fear God.
²⁰ My companion stretched out his hand against his friends;
he violated his covenant.
²¹ His speech was smooth as butter,
yet war was in his heart;
his words were softer than oil,
yet they were drawn swords.
²² Cast your burden on the LORD,
and he will sustain you he will never permit
the righteous to be moved.
²³ But you, O God, will cast them down
into the pit of destruction;

men of blood and treachery
shall not live out half their days.
But I will trust in you. (Psalm 55 ESV)

Bibliography

Achtemeier, Paul. *Romans. Interpretation. A Bible Commentary for Teaching and Preaching.* Louisville: John Knox Press, 1985.

Adams, Jay. *Handbook of Church Discipline: A Right and Privilege of Every Church Member.* Grand Rapids: Zondervan, 1974.

_____. *Language of Counseling.* Stanley: Timeless Texts, 1981.

American Association of Christian Counselors. "Mission," http://www.aacc.net/about-us/ (accessed April 6, 2015).

Amos, Clare. *The Book of Genesis.* Werrington: Biddles Ltd., 2004.

Antai,Diddy. "Controlling behavior, power relations within intimate relationships and intimate partner physical and sexual violence against women in Nigeria." *BMC Public Health* 11:511(2011). http://www.biomedcentral.com/1471-2458/11/511 (accessed November 10, 2014).

Arnold, Bill. *Genesis. The New Cambridge Bible Commentary.* New York: Cambridge University Press, 2009.

Balswick, Judith and Jack Balswick. "Marriage as a Partnership of Equals." In *Discovering Biblical Equality: Complementarity Without Hierarchy.* edited by Ronald Pierce and Rebecca Groothuis448-463. Downers Grove: Inter-varsity Press, 2005.

Belleville, Linda. "Women in Ministry: An Egalitarian Perspective." In *Two Views on Women in Ministry,* edited by James Beck and Linda Belleville, 19-119. Grand Rapids: Zondervan, 2005.

_____. *Women Leaders and the Church.* Grand Rapids: Baker Books, 2000.

Berkhof, Louis. *Systematic Theology.* 15th ed. Edinburgh: The Banner of Truth Trust, 2000.

Blomberg, Craig. *1 Corinthians. The NIV Application Commentary.* Grand Rapids: Zondervan Publishing House, 1994.

_____. "Women in Ministry: A Complementarian Perspective." In *Two Views on Women in Ministry,* edited by James Beck and Linda Belleville 123-184. Grand Rapids: Zondervan, 2005.

Bordwine, James. *The Pauline Doctrine of Male Headship. The Apostle versus Biblical Feminists.* Greenville: Greenville Seminary Press, 1996.

Briscoe, D. *The Preacher's Commentary: Genesis* Nashville: Thomas Nelson Publishers, 1987.

Bruce, F.F. *The Epistle to the Colossians to Philemon and to the Ephesians.* Grand Rapids: Wm. Eerdmans Publishing Co., 1984.

_____. *The Epistle to the Ephesians.* London: Pickering &Inglis, Ltd., 1961.

Brueggeman, Walter. *Genesis. A Bible Commentary for Teaching and Preaching.* Atlanta: John Knox Press, 1982.

Cloud, Henry, & John Townsend. *Boundaries: When to Say Yes. When to Say No to Take Control of Your Life.* Grand Rapids: Zondervan, 1992.

Davids, Peter. *Ephesians, Philippians, Colossians, 1-2 Thessalonians, Philemon. Cornerstone Biblical Commentary.* Edited by Philip Comfort. Carol Stream: Tyndale House Publishers, 2008.

_____. "A Silent Witness in Marriage: 1 Peter 3:1-7." In *Discovering Biblical Equality: Complementarity Without Hierarchy.* edited by Ronald Pierce and Rebecca Groothuis, 224-238. Downers Grove: Inter-varsity Press, 2005.

Davidson, R. *Genesis 1-11. The Cambridge Bible Commentary on the New English Bible.* Cambridge University Press, 1973.

Ellis, Albert, and Marcia Powers. *The Secret of Overcoming Verbal Abuse: Getting Off the Emotional Roller Coaster and Regaining Control of Your Life.* Hollywood: Wilshire Book Company, 2000.

Engel, Beverly. *The Emotionally Abused Woman: Overcoming Destructive Patterns and Reclaiming Yourself.* New York: Fawcett Books, 1990.

_____. *The Emotionally Abusive Relationship: How to Stop Being Abused and How to Stop Abusing.* Hoboken: John Wiley & Sons Inc., 2002.

Erickson, Millard. *Christian Theology.* 13th ed. Grand Rapids: Baker Book House, 1985.

Evans, Patricia. *The Verbally Abusive Relationship: How to Recognize it and How to Respond.* Avon, MA: Adams Media, 2010.

Eyrich, Howard and William Hines. *Curing the Heart: A Model for Biblical Counseling.* Fearn: Christian Focus Publications Ltd., 2002.

Fitzpatrick, Elyse. "Christ's Word to Worriers." *Institute for Counseling and Discipleship.* Summer Institute 2011, mp3.

_____. *Helper by Design: God's Perfect Plan for Women in Marriage.* Chicago: Moody Publishers, 2003.

Follingstad, Diane and Dana Dehart. "Defining Psychological Abuse of Husbands Toward Wives Contexts, Behaviors, and Typologies." *Journal of Interpersonal Violence* 15, no. 9 (September 2000): 891-920.

Frame, John. "Men and Women in the Image of God," In *Recovering Biblical Manhood and Womanhood,* edited by John Piper and Wayne Grudem, 228-236. Wheaton: Crossway Books, 1991.

Gaebelein, Frank. *The Expositor's Bible Commentary. Genesis, Exodus, Leviticus, Numbers.* Grand Rapids: Zondervan Publishing House, 1990.

Galloway, Sid. "Wife Abuse." *National Association of Nouthetic Counselors.* Annual Conference 1992. CD N9209.

Gispen, W. *Commentaar op het Oude Testament: Genesis 1-11.* Kampen: J.H. Kok, 1974.

Goode, Wm. "Wife Abuse (90)." *National Association of Nouthetic Counselors.* Annual Conference 1990. CD N9027.

Groothuis, Rebecca. "Equal in Being, Unequal in Role: Exploring the Logic of Women's Subordination." In *Discovering Biblical Equality: Complementarity Without Hierarchy,* edited by Ronald Pierce and Rebecca Groothuis, 301-333. Downers Grove: Inter-varsity Press, 2005.

Grudem, Wayne. "The Key Issues in the Manhood and Womanhood Controversy, And The Way Forward." In *Biblical Foundations for Manhood and Womanhood,* edited by Wayne Grudem, 19-68. Wheaton: Crossway Books, 2002.

_____. *Systematic Theology: An Introduction to Biblical Doctrine.* Leicester: Inter-varsity Press, 1994.

Hay, David. *Colossians.* Nashville: Abingdon Press, 2000.

Hendrickson, Laura. "Counseling Victims of Spousal Abuse." *Institute for Biblical Counseling & Discipleship*. mp3. http://www.ibcd.org/resources/messages/counseling-victims-of-spousal-abuse/ (accessed January 16, 2014).

Hendrikson, William. *New Testament Commentary: Exposition of Colossians and Philemon.* Grand Rapids: Baker Book House, 1975.

Hess, Richard. "Equality With and Without Innocence: Genesis 1-3." In *Discovering Biblical Equality: Complementarity Without Hierarchy,* edited by Ronald Pierce and Rebecca Groothuis, 481-493. Downers Grove: Inter-varsity Press, 2005.

Hirigoyen, Marie-France. *Stalking the Soul: Emotional Abuse and the Erosion of Identity.* New York: Helen Marx Books, 2004.

Holcomb Justin and Lindsay Holcomb. *Rid of My Disgrace: Hope and Healing for Victims of Sexual Assault.* Wheaton: Crossway, 2011.

Horsley, Richard. *1 Corinthians.* Nashville: Abingdon Press, 1998.

Hunt, June. *How to Rise Above Abuse: Victory for Victims of Five Types of Abuse.* Eugene: Harvest House Publishers, 2010.

Hurley, James. *Man and Women in Biblical Perspective.* Leicester: Inter-varsity Press, 2005.

Jackson, Tim. "Emotionally Destructive Marriages." *RBC Webinars,* May 3rd 2014. http://helpformylife.org/2014/03/05/the-emotionally-destructive-marriage-webinar (accessed July 13, 2014).

Kelleman, Robert. "Counseling and Abuse in Marriage." *RPM Ministries.* Pdf.

_____. *Sexual Abuse: Beauty for Ashes.* Phillipsburg: P&R Publishing, 2013.

Kimball, Cynthia. "Nature, Culture, and Gender Complementarity," In *Discovering Biblical Equality: Complementarity Without Hierarchy,* edited by Ronald Pierce and Rebecca Groothuis 464-480. Downers Grove: Inter-varsity Press, 2005.

Kistemaker, Simon. *1 Corinthians. New Testament Commentary.* Grand Rapids: Zondervan Publishing House, 1994.

Knight, George. "The Family and the Church: How Should Biblical Manhood and Womanhood Work Out in Practice?" In *Recovering Biblical Manhood and Womanhood,* edited by John Piper and Wayne Grudem, 161-175. Wheaton: Crossway Books, 1991.

_____. "Husbands and Wives as Analogies of Christ and the Church. Ephesians 5:21-33 and Colossians 3:18-19." In *Recovering Biblical Manhood and Womanhood.* edited by John Piper and Wayne Grudem, 161-175. Wheaton: Crossway Books, 1991.

Liefield, Walter. "The Nature of Authority in the New Testament." In *Discovering Biblical Equality: Complementarity Without Hierarchy,* edited by Ronald Pierce and Rebecca Groothuis, 255-271. Downers Grove: Inter-varsity Press, 2005.

Loring, Marti. *Emotional Abuse.* San Francisco: Jossey-Bass Publishers, 1994.

MacArthur, John. *Galatians.* Chicago: The Moody Press, 1987.

Mack, Wayne. "Biblical Help for Overcoming Despondency, Depression." *The Journal of Pastoral Practice* II, no. 2. (1978): 31-48.

———. "Loneliness & Self-Pity#1: How to Handle Loneliness." *The Dr. Wayne Mack Library.* CDWM4191.

Marshall, I. "Mutual Love and Submission in Marriage. Colossians 3:18-19 and Ephesians 5:21-33." In *Discovering Biblical Equality: Complementarity Without Hierarchy,* edited by Ronald Pierce and Rebecca Groothuis, 186-204. Downers Grove: Inter-varsity Press, 2005.

Matteus, Kenneth. *Genesis 1-11: 26. Vol 1A. An Exegetical & Theological Exposition Holy Scripture. The New American Commentary.* Nashville: B&H Publishing Group, 1996.

Mercadante, Linda. *From Hierarchy to Equality: A Comparison of Past and Present Interpretations of 1 Corinthians 11:2-16 in Relation to the Changing Status of Women in Society.* Vancouver: Regent College, 1978.

Miller, Mary. *No Visible Wounds: Identifying Nonphysical Abuse of Women by their Men.* New York: Ballantine Books, 1995.

Mounce, Robert. *Romans. The New American Commentary. An Exegetical and Theological Exposition of Holy Scripture* (Nashville: Broadman and Holman Publishers, 1995), 149.

Needham, Robert. "Abuse: Addressing It." *Institute for Biblical Counseling & Discipleship.* mp3. February 10th, 2013. http:ibcd.org/resources/messages/cdc1-14-1angerabuse/ (accessed January 16, 2014).

———. "Abuse: Recognizing It." *Institute for Biblical Counseling & Discipleship.* mp3. http://www.soundword.com/ab1reitm.html (accessed January 16, 2014).

Neuer, Werner. *Man & Woman in Christian Perspective.* London: Hodder & Stoughton, 1990.

Newheiser, Jim. "Anger/Abuse." *Institute for Biblical Counseling & Discipleship,* mp3, February 10th, 2013. http://www.ibcd.org/resources/messages/cdc1-14-angerabuse/ (accessed January 16, 2014).

_____. "Church Discipline: 1 Corinthians 5." *Institute for Biblical Counseling & Discipleship.* mp3.

Newheiser, Caroline. "Helping Women who are Married but Lonely." *The Institute for Biblical Counseling and Discipleship.* Summer Institute 2013. mp3.

NiCarthy, Ginny. *Getting Free: A Handbook for Women in Abusive Situations.* Worcester: Billing & Sons, Ltd., 1991).

Nicole, Roger. "Biblical Hermeneutics: Basic Principles and Questions of Gender." In *Discovering Biblical Equality: Complementarity Without Hierarchy,* edited by Ronald Pierce and Rebecca Groothuis, 355-363. Downers Grove: Intervarsity Press, 2005.

Nicols, Brittney. "Violence Against Women: The Extent of the Problem." In *"Intimate Violence Against Women: When Spouses, Partners, or Lovers Attack.* edited by Paula Lundberg-Love and Shelly Marmion, 1-8. Westport: Praeger Publishers, 2006.

Novsak, Rachel., Tina Mandelj, and Barbara Simonic. "Therapeutic Implications of Religious- Related Emotional Abuse." *Journal of Aggression, Maltreatment, & Trauma* Vol. 21, Issue 1 (2012): 31-44.

O'Brien, Peter. *Colossians, Philemon. Word Biblical Commentary.* Waco: Word Books, 1982.

_____. *The Letter to the Ephesians. Pillar The New Testament Commentary* (Leicester: Apollos, 1999.

Ortland, Raymond. "Male-Female Equality and Headship: Genesis 1-3." In *Recovering Biblical Manhood and Womanhood,* edited by John Piper and Wayne Grudem, 86-104. Wheaton: Crossway Books, 1991.

Osbourne, Grant. ed. *Romans. The I.V.P. New Testament Commentary Series.* Downers Grove: Intervarsity Press, 2004.

Oxford Concise English Dictionary of Current English 9th ed.(New York: Oxford University Press, 1995.

Patzia, Arthur. *Ephesians, Colossians, Philemon. New International Biblical Commentary.* Peabody: Hendrickson, 1990.

Pieters, Jerome et al. "Emotional, Physical, and Sexual Abuse: The Experiences of Men and Women." *Institute for the Equality of Men and Women.* http ://igvm-iefh.belgium.be. (Accessed November 10, 2014).

Piper, John. "An Overview of Critical Concerns: Questions and Answers." In *Recovering Biblical Manhood and Womanhood,* edited by John Piper and Wayne Grudem, 25-55. Wheaton: Crossway Books, 1991.

_____. "A Vision of Biblical Complementarity: Manhood and Womanhood Defined According to the Bible." In *Recovering Biblical Manhood and Womanhood,* edited by John Piper and Wayne Grudem, 25-55. Wheaton: Crossway Books, 1991.

Powlison, David. "The River of Life Flows Through the Slough of Despond." *The Journal of Biblical Counseling,* 18, no. 2 (Winter 2000), 2-4.

Priolo, Lou. "Biblical Resources for the Wife's Protection." *The Lou Priolo Audio Library.* CD LP40.

———. "Counseling Angry People." *The Institute for Biblical Counseling & Discipleship,* mp3, June 26th, 2008. http://www.ibcd.org/resources/messages/counseling-angry-people/ (accessed January 17, 2014).

———. "Helping People Pleasers." *National Association of Nouthetic Counselors.* Conference 2006. mp3.

———. "How to Respond to Rejection and Hurt." *The Lou Priolo Library.* CD LP52b.

Pryde, Debi, & Robert Needham. *A Biblical Perspective of What to Do When You are Abused by Your Husband.* New Springs: Iron Sharpeneth Iron Publications, 2003.

Rinck, Margaret. *Christian Men who Hate Women.* Grand Rapids: Zondervan, 1990.

Ross, Allen. *Genesis. Cornerstone Biblical Commentary.* Carol Stream, Illinois: Tyndale House Publishers, 2008.

Ryken, Leland, James Wilhoit, and Tremper Longman. ed. *Dictionary of Biblical Imagery: An encyclopedic exploration of the images, symbols, motifs, metaphors, figures of speech and literary patterns of the Bible.* Downers Grove: InterVarsity Press USA.

Ryken, Philip. *Galatians. Reformed Expository Commentary.* Phillipsburg: P&R Publishing, 2005.

Sande, Ken. "Redemptive Church Discipline." *Institute for Biblical Counseling & Discipleship.* Summer Institute. 2009. mp3.

Scheckter, Sarah. "Emotionally Abusive Relationships." *Perelman School of Medicine, Department of Psychiatry Penn Behavioral Health* http://www/med.upenn.edu/psychotherapy/Schechter--EmotionallyAbusive.html (accessed January 8, 2014).

Schreiner, Thomas. "Women in Ministry: Another Complementarian Perspective." In *Two Views on Women in Ministry,* edited by James Beck and Linda Belleville, 265-342. Grand Rapids: Zondervan, 2005.

Scipione, George. "How to Counsel Spousal Abuse." *National Association of Nouthetic Counselors.* Conference 1999. CD N9938.

_____. "Worry." *CCEF – West San Diego 92.* CD ibc9233.

Somerville, Mary. "Coping with Loneliness." *National Association of Nouthetic Counselors*, Annual Conference, 2005, mp3.

Spencer, Aida. "Jesus' Treatment of Women in the Gospels." In *Discovering Biblical Equality: Complementarity Without Hierarchy,* edited by Ronald Pierce and Rebecca Groothuis, 126-141. Downers Grove: Inter-varsity Press, 2005.

Stark, Evan. *Coercive Control: How Men Entrap Women in Personal Life.* New York: Oxford University Press, 2007.

Storkey, Elaine. *Created or Constructed: The Great Gender Debate.* Carlisle: Paternoster Press, 2000.

Stott, John. *The Message of Galatians. The Bible Speaks Today.* Leicester: Inter-Varsity Press, 1968.

_____. *The Message of 1 Timothy & Titus: The Bible Speaks Today.* Leicester: Inter-varsity Press, 1996.

Street, John. "Handle with Care: Counseling Abuse Victims." *National Association of Nouthetic Counselors* Conference 2012, mp3.

The Biblical Counseling Coalition. "Confessional Statement." http://biblicalcounselingcoalition.org/about/confessional-statement/ (accessed May 31, 2014).

Tracy, Steven. *Mending the Soul: Understanding and Healing Abuse.* Grand Rapids: Zondervan, 2005.

United Nations. "International Day for the Elimination of Violence Against Women." http://www.un.org/en/events/endviolenceday/ (accessed May 31, 2014).

Uprichard, Richard. *Ephesians. An EP Commentary.* Auburn: Evangelical Press, 2004.

Vernick, Leslie. *The Emotionally Destructive Marriage.* Colorado Springs: WaterBrook Press, 2013.

_____. *How to Act Right When Your Spouse Acts Wrong.* Colorado Springs: WaterBrook Press, 2001.

Wall, Robert. *Colossians and Philemon. The IVP New Testament Commentary Series.* Downers Grove: Intervarsity Press, 1993.

Ware, Bruce. "Male and Female Complementarity and the Image of God." In *Biblical Foundations for Manhood and Womanhood,* edited by Wayne Grudem, 71-92. Wheaton: Crossway Books, 2002.

Welch, Ed. *Blame it on the Brain: Distinguishing Chemical Imbalances, Brain Disorders, and Disobedience.* Phillipsburg: P&R Publishing, 1998.

_____. "Boundaries in Relationships," *The Journal of Biblical Counseling* 23, no. 3 (January 2004):15-24.

_____. "Counseling Those Who Are Depressed," *The Journal of Biblical Counseling* 18, no. 2 (Winter 2000):5-7.

_____. *Depression: Looking Up from the Stubborn Darkness.* Greensboro: New Growth Press, 2011.

_____. "Helping Those Who Are Depressed." *The Journal of Biblical Counseling* 18, no. 2 (Winter 2000): 25-31.

_____. *Shame Interrupted: How God Lifts the Pain of Worthlessness & Rejection* Greensboro: New Growth Press, 2012.

_____. "Understanding Depression." *The Journal of Biblical Counseling* 18, no. 2 (Winter 2000): 12-24.

_____. *When People are Big and God is Small: Overcoming Peer Pressure, Codependency, and the Fear of Man.* Phillipsburg: P&R Publishing, 1997.

_____. "Words of Hope for Those Who Struggle with Depression." *The Journal of Biblical Counseling* 18, no. 2 (Winter 2000): 40-46.

Wenham, Gordon. *Genesis 1-15. Word Biblical Commentary.* Waco: Word Books Publishers, 1987.

Westwood, Tom. *Colossians.* Redlands: Bible Treasury Hour Inc., 1970.

Wright, R. "God, Metaphor and Gender: Is the God of the Bible a Male Deity?" In *Discovering Biblical Equality: Complementarity Without Hierarchy,* edited by Ronald Pierce and Rebecca Groothuis287-300. Downers Grove: Intervarsity Press, 2005.

Made in the USA
Coppell, TX
04 February 2022